T3-AJJ-958

Leading for success

Leading for success

The seven sides to great leaders

Andrew Kakabadse
Nada Kakabadse
and
Linda Lee-Davies

First published 2008 by
PALGRAVE MACMILLAN

Palgrave Macmillan in the UK is an imprint of Macmillan Publishers Limited, registered in England, company number 785998, of Houndmills, Basingstoke, Hampshire RG21 6XS.

Palgrave Macmillan in the US is a division of St Martin's Press LLC, 175 Fifth Avenue, New York, NY 10010.

Palgrave Macmillan is the global academic imprint of the above companies and has companies and representatives throughout the world.

Palgrave® and Macmillan® are registered trademarks in the United States, the United Kingdom, Europe and other countries.

ISBN-13: 978–0–230–53715–6
ISBN-10: 0–230–53715–4

This book is printed on paper suitable for recycling and made from fully managed and sustained forest sources. Logging, pulping and manufacturing processes are expected to conform to the environmental regulations of the country of origin.

A catalogue record for this book is available from the British Library.

A catalog record for this book is available from the Library of Congress.

10 9 8 7 6 5 4 3 2 1
17 16 15 14 13 12 11 10 09 08

Printed and bound in China

CONTENTS

LIST OF FIGURES AND TABLES

Figures

Tables

Our deepest thanks to Madeleine Fleure and Sheena Darby for their patience and perseverance in preparing script after script to produce this text. Thanks also to Peter Parkes, Glasshouse Partnership, for adding that elegant touch to the diagrams and figures in this book.

Also this book, as with so many other studies and publications, has been made possible through the generosity of the senior managers of the Severstal Corporation. In particular, our thanks to Alexei Mordashov, Vadim Makhov, Dmitry Afanasyev, and Dmitry Kouptsov.

Further, we are particularly grateful for the time given and the interest shown by our top business and public service leader colleagues, who shared with us their thoughts and experiences that led to their success. It is these best practices that is the heart of this book in particular we would like to thank.

Dr Hans Blix, Former head of UN weapons inspections in Iraq, former Director-General of the International Atomic Energy Agency, and former Foreign Minister of Sweden.

Rona Cant, Explorer, Adventurer, and Keynote Speaker.

Steven Crawshaw, CEO Bradford & Bingley Plc, Bingley, West Yorkshire.

Viscount Etienne Davignon, Chairman of the European Academy of Business in Society, company Chairman, one of the key founders of the European Union, Belgium.

Olivier Giscard d'Estaing, Chairman of the European League for Economic Cooperation and the Committee for a World Parliament (COPAM), Founder and Chairman, European

Institute of Business Administration, Former member of the French Parliament, France.

Val Gooding, CEO, BUPA, London, UK.

Baroness Maggic Jones, House of Lords, London, UK, ex-Unison, Trustee of Shelter.

Dannie Joste, Executive Leadership Consultant, Switzerland.

Lord Tom Sawyer, House of Lords, London, UK.

Dr. Bernd Scheifele, Chairman of the Managing Board, HeidelbergCement AG, Heidelberg, Germany.

Vanni Treves, Chairman, Korn/Ferry International (UK), London.

Sister Judith Zoebelin, Franciscan Sister of the Eucharist, and the founder of the Holy See's World Wide WebSite.

Then there are all those who contributed to the research underlying this book and to the book itself. Although nameless, your contribution is deeply appreciated.

It has been the intention of the authors throughout this text to create original ideas and develop original models based on their own experience as well as the input from the named contributors. To this end the direct use of academic texts has been avoided. They would, however, like to acknowledge the following few texts/papers for their influence on the direction of the work.

Cranwell-Ward, J., Bacon A., and Mackie, R. (2002) *Inspiring Leadership*, London: Thomson Learning.

Hamel, G. and Prahalad, C.K. (1996) *Competing for the Future*, Boston: Harvard Business School Press.

Handy, C. (1999) *The New Alchemists*, London: Hutchinson.

Hooper, A. and Potter, J. (2001) *Intelligent Leadership*, UK: Random House.

Johnson, G., Scholes, K., and Whittington, R. (2006) *Exploring Corporate Strategy*, FT Prentice Hall, Harlow, Essex, UK.

Kakabadse, A. and Kakabadse, N. (1999) *Essence of Leadership*, London: International Thomson Business Press.

Kakabadse, A., Kakabadse, N., and Lee-Davies, L. (2005) "Visioning the Pathway: A Leadership Process Model," *European Management Journal*, 23(2): 237–246.

Lee-Davies, L., Kakabadse, N., and Kakabadse, A. (2007) "Shared Leadership: Leading through Polylogue," *Business Strategy Series*, 8(4): 246–253.

Mullins, L. (2006) *Essentials of Organisational Behaviour*, FT Prentice Hall.

Yukl, G. (2002) *Leadership in Organisations*, FT Prentice Hall.

Andrew Kakabadse Professor of International Management Development, Cranfield School of Management. Andrew was the H. Smith Richardson Fellow at CCL, North Carolina, USA and is Visiting Professor at the University of Ulster; Macquarie Graduate School of Management; Thunderbird and at Swinburne University. His research covers boards, top teams, and the governance of governments. He has published 26 books, 169 articles, and 16 monographs.

Andrew is coeditor of *The Journal of Management Development* and *Corporate Governance: International Journal of Business in Society*.

a.p.kakabadse@cranfield.ac.uk

Nada Kakabadse BSc. Grad. Dip., MSc. MPA., Ph.D. is currently Professor in Management and Business research at the University of Northampton Business School and the coeditor (with Andrew Kakabadse) of *The Journal of Management Development* and *Corporate Governance: International Journal of Business in Society*. Nada has published widely in areas of leadership, application of IS/IT corporations, corporate governance, government, Boardroom effectivness, diversity management and ethics, including 10 books, 51 chapters in international volumes, 3 monographs and over 100 scholarly and reviewed articles. Nada has acted as a consultant to numerous public and private sector organizations.

nada.kakabadse@northampton.ac.uk

Linda Lee-Davies BA (Hons) MBA – Senior Lecturer in Business and International Management. Linda lectures at The University of Northampton and heads the commercial, part-time management suite through to and including MBA. With a keen interest in leadership and its links to strategic change, as well as a passion for promoting executive personal development planning, she particularly focuses on working with business clients to keep material relevant and useful to the workplace.

linda.lee-davies@northampton.ac.uk

The seven sides of great leaders

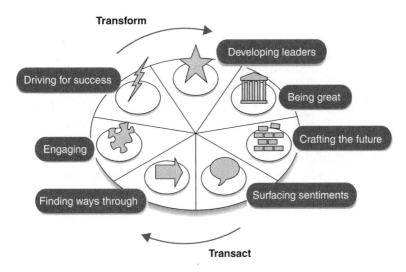

Source: Authors

Countries, Companies, and Cultures rise and fall because of their leaders. Who a leader is and what a leader does defines the future success or failure of all in their custody.

Great leading men and women – good and bad – have come and gone in history. In great demand one minute and out of time, fashion, and favor the next. Life patterns, land boundaries, and culture today have been patterned by historical figures such as the hard-headed hero Hannibal and even the greedy, geography gaining Genghis Khan. Morals and standards have been set by figures such as the generous, giving Gandhi and the diplomatic, discerning Australian Premier, Kevin Rudd. More currently the matriarchal

messages of Maggie T or the bumbling benchmarks of Bush contribute to the confusion of where greatness actually comes from.
All different in their influence, all different in their use of power –
no one character or method would seem to be the definitive driving
force of success.

Leadership then is most accurately defined in context. Different
situations bring about the need for different actions and reactions
by all, so it follows that the followers need a different type of leadership appropriate to their particular circumstances of the time.

One-size–fits-all is out

Leadership survival in today's volatile economic climate is by
default itself a volatile condition. It must be ever changing to
keep pace with, match, and predict the surprises likely to be put
upon it. A linear definition of leadership one minute means
nothing the next so it is futile trying to state that leadership is
one particular trait, one particular character, or one particular
style. It is limiting to channel leadership definition through only
one of the participating parties in the equation when all have
their effect on it – from the individual leading to the individual
nature and needs of the followers. Context commands the category of behavior or action, so a great leader must have a number
of personalities or sides available to them to be able to fit most
appropriately to any situation they face.

The tailored leadership suit is in

These personalities must be different but linked, and a great
leader will work on having a range of available suits. In the same
way we change our clothes for different occasions, the leader
will change their particular offering to provide the right support
for their followers. This book looks at the capsule wardrobe that
they need to invest in.

This approach then suggests that one person is capable of being
a great leader not just in one climate but in many climates and
that it is not always necessary to change the leader every time
the organizational weather changes. Organizations can benefit

from continuity and experience if the same leader can change in line with the climate. The leader too benefits from a wider portfolio of skills at their disposal. Leadership shelf-life expectancy is extended if one is able to chameleon in karma yoga (altruistic action to achieve perfection).

The leadership sides necessary for success must embrace a cocktail of leadership and management techniques which from a pivotal point of personal greatness creates the future of the organization by grasping the vision and bringing it to ground level. Long-term vision is punctuated by the ability to manage and motivate teams, manage resources, and ensure synergy at all levels to maximize organizational and individual potential. Being great may be the start but yet it is also the sum of six other key parts of the great leader package. The chapter opening figure shows the interlinking yet very different seven sides of great leaders.

Indeed, it is about a portfolio of skills and attributes but, importantly, also the way in which they are used to create the synergy. Extra output is achieved by careful thought and consideration for all aspects of the leadership influence. The influence is more about predicting and reacting to the situation and individual as well as corporate need appropriately, thus providing the right service, support, and direction.

Leadership is not about acting or being big through positional power or any other – we can all appear big in Lilliput! Lilliputian leadership gets its 15 minutes of fame in some companies, but without a rounded set of leadership skills to choose from as the environment dictates, shelf life decreases dramatically as the enormity of change dwarfs the foolish culprit.

Leadership theory has historically attributed effectiveness or greatness to particular components of the leader themselves, the situation, or the followers. What we are now saying here is that there are different sides to the great leadership personality but they are used at different times and in different quantity as appropriate. They are, however, always there to draw on and one does not outweigh another in the overall balance.

Equally, once a leader is given the privilege of power, how they use it and with what discretion are also key to success. Discretionary leadership is formed by these discretionary choices. Being able to choose the appropriate action for a particular situation is a science in itself. Being able to be the appropriate leader for the moment is an art in itself.

So it is not just about having the right skills at one's disposal, but also about being able to select them to fit the situation and context which takes discerning discretionary judgment.

The seven sides of great leaders

The seven sides of great leaders have been selected in a discretionary way. Extensive author experience in the field and many personal field observations at high impact levels across commercial and public sector disciplines have provided a very wide choice of direction to take. These have been carefully considered to decide the chosen defining factors of successful leadership and raise matters for discussion. This rests on the firm foundation of in-depth international research drawn from the contribution of many working teams within international management development center environments.

Classic leadership theory is presented in a fresh and fashionable framework for discussion in a practical book for managers written in a journalistic way. Do not be deceived though by the easy to read style, this book is securely underpinned with the most credible and extensive research. Many thousands of executives have been interviewed in depth and questionnaired at length across twenty or more countries. Further more, well over four hundred boards have been scrutinized as well as the federal government of Australia, the public services of Scotland, and an array of public organizations and health services around the globe. In addition to this impressive pedigree of strong but subtle academic structure, top level case studies and frank opinion from prominent business and political leaders have been threaded throughout to bring the book to life.

Quotes from great leaders such as, Viscount Davignon – one of the founders of the European Union; Lord Tom Sawyer – renowned Trade Union Leader; Baroness Maggie Jones – Social Activist;

Hans Blix – the Weapons Inspector of Iraq; Val Gooding – CEO of BUPA; Rona Cant – Adventurer; Steven Crawshaw, CEO of Bradford and Bingley; Sister Judith Zeobelin – Founder of the Holy See's World Wide Website; Dr. Bernd Scheifele – Chairman HeidelbergCement; Vanni Treves, Chairman Korn/Ferry International; Olivier Giscard d'Estaing – Chairman of INSEAD; and Dannie Jost – Executive Leadership Consultant ensure a rounded insight into this turbulent topic. The sheer breadth of national and international experiences which surfaces in the contributions from this wide range of "great" leaders really stirs up thought within the reader.

"Case Study Comments" from this wide selection have been chosen to give the necessary punch of reality and reflect different working situations and attached to the appropriate "side" to illustrate the discussion raised.

"Walk the Talk" stepping stones have been placed in each chapter. These very frankly and directly address the issues in debate. From lively and rounded discussion, the reader is immediately drawn to positive action by probing and sometimes quite personal questions as well as definite tasks. These "Case Study Comments" and "Walk the Talk" stepping stones also provide a glance mechanism through the chapters and give a flavor of the issues in their own right.

The seven sides

Being great

Something within the leader is key to them being great. It may not be a particular characteristic or style but perhaps a perceptive or receptive ability to be the right thing at the right time. Personality, elements of narcissism, character, and experience may all play a part in making up the leader package but it is the manifestation of leadership discretion and choice which ensures that the outcome of decisions are the correct ones and it is this appropriate output which is the true barometer of their greatness. Being great is one of the seven sides of great leaders and to be so the other six play their part. Being great is also therefore the encapsulation of all of the sides of great leaders and operates at two levels – initiating the choice of sides to use and terminating in the culmination of those choices.

Crafting the future

From within the leader themselves, and indeed using that "being great" element they have, they create and set the vision. Blessed with the character and ability to inspire, the great leader ensures and indeed crafts the future in such a way that all have a clear direction in which to travel. Creating that vision requires business expertise and the ability to predict. Even more than that, the great leader then brings that future to the organization in real and understandable terms. At the same time as evangelizing the excitement of the way forward, the great leader is translating the overall strategy into manageable tactics.

So the elements of crafting the future cover a range of skills. Determining the future is a priority. The key element of setting such strategic direction is not an isolated one though. Such vision is the creation of the future, not the crafting of it. The crafting of the future is made up of a set of sub-elements which bring that vision about. In addition to a personal conviction to the created vision there must exist the leadership elements which link all levels of the team from front line to top management. Communication must also be conducive to cooperation and promote a feedback culture which keeps fresh information flowing to the top and so increases the likelihood of correct decision making.

Surfacing sentiments

None of this is possible without being astute and clever in terms of what is going on at ground level and beyond. Understanding the workings of the front line or the shop floor is of course essential but the extra and invisible power of synergy is only available to those who look further than that and the obvious. It is not just about selling in the ideas with dramatic evangelization of the dream and inviting comment, it is about truly penetrating the intangible layers of dynamics, sentiments, and emotion which are not readily visible – especially from an ivory tower.

Token empowerments of yesteryear surfaced only a cosmetic level of feeling from a workforce because the concern itself was only administered at a cosmetic level. In order to surface sentiments most effectively, the great leader must drill deeper and this is less about rolling sleeves up at the front line and more about rolling true feelings out from the heart. This will only occur in the right atmosphere of trust and once underway will educate the leader with the real spirit of what is actually going on under their nose rather than risk being fed with what followers think they want to hear.

Understanding team dynamics and politics will bring more productivity through overt trust and enlightenment and this in turn will drive less underground where covert, hidden agendas can surface as sabotage.

Hidden agendas exist at every level so a key element of surfacing sentiments is ensuring all parties clear the air and feel able to trust the leader's fair treatment of and use of the views given. The shared views in turn give way to the element of shared leadership where shared responsibility for actions makes way for true empowerment.

Finding ways through

From the inner core of the leader to the vision of the future, to delving deep into the emotions of the workforce to gain their following, we get down to the brass tacks of the basic strategy for actually managing the enterprise. Ensuring the correct structures and design of the framework of the company will support and push toward the overall strategic direction. In addition to working with the invisible above in surfacing sentiments, the visible needs attention. Organizational culture needs to be in line with not only the overall vision but also the actual needs of the individuals themselves, for instance. The flexibility and agility of the company must be tuned to meet visioning need so all day-to-day activities fit in with and are in line with the one direction that the organization is going in. Choice of pathway is as difficult as choice of leadership style to use at any particular moment and conflict of interests is a possibility where the ideal is confronted by reality. Ethical dilemmas will occur where the two are not in line.

Transactional management thus is a part of great leadership and this part furnishes the mechanics of the business or service. It is evident though that it is not merely the practice of getting things done at ground level which is important but the pressure of leadership choice or discretion which dictates the level of success of the activities. This seems to suggest that this element is not only a part of being great as a leader but also that great leadership exists at all and different levels of the business.

Engaging

Empowerment and beyond! Here we enter the territory of real ownership. Having transformationally tuned in to the needs of the individuals and teams and extracted synergetic output with that skill, it is important to leave the workforce with a true bond between them and the organization. This then comes back to different levels and types of communication and turning transformation information gained at the emotional level to transaction action at the practical one. Employees not only need to know what to do but they also need to know why they are doing it and where it fits into the bigger picture. They also need to be able to input into the decisions as to what is appropriate and why at this level.

Only with the allowance of autonomy comes a true sense of responsibility and therefore a true accountability to the company. The "them and us" environment breaks down as dialogue, in fact a multiple dialogue; let us call it a polylogue. So polylogue or multiple discussion is encouraged and transparent at all levels and more useful information, more likely to assist the business, is passed through the ranks and contributes more effectively to the decision-making process. This occurs more naturally because the great leader exacts their positional power in a much more referent form and makes sure that they not only facilitate a polylogue but also ensure that they are a true link between followers and corporate need.

Where choice of activity was the theme in the previous leadership side, the choice of spin, ideas, branding, communication, and presentation becomes the theme here. This makes the difference between getting followers to do things because they have to and because they want to. The creation of desire not only involves inclusion but also an ability to appeal to the follower at the right level without being too ambitious and without being condescending.

Driving for success

Once the future is created, the followers psychologically analyzed, the choices of activity made, and the appropriate communication in progress the work has only just begun. Getting there is one thing – staying there is quite another.

Staying power has got to be another facet of the great leader and the stamina to stick it out is no accident. Make no mistake, we are not just talking about the staying power of the leader themselves and the extent of their shelf life, although that is very important, but also of the systems, processes, ideas, and vision that they have put in place. Performance must be maintained and managed and perhaps even pushed. Success must be driven. This should be achieved with a complete buy in from the followers and without getting to a point of burn out.

Performance measurement is necessary with scientific audit of progress, a standard and respected part of forward thinking leadership leaning, rather than a ridiculed inspection of events. Internal controls need to be in place, so regular checks on actual performance against those desired or predicted are made. Even more importantly, these need to be assessed at every level to ensure that they are not only meeting the strategic need but also fulfilling and developing the individuals and teams producing the results.

The performance measurement and management we are talking about here is not a short-term check against a short-term target but a three-dimensional perspective of how all activities contribute to long-term events and where benchmarking is used in a positive feedback culture. In addition to setting up and sustaining processes and systems or targets and incentives within an umbrella of audit to generate, inspire, and maintain organizational competence it is also necessary to ensure the personal development and satisfaction of those whose hands the activities are in. Staying power is only possible if the tasks the followers are given are suitable to their capability and motivate and improve them in some way. As the followers "churn out" the output, the great leader has to consider their "learn out" point so that they are not under or over used according to their particular and individual levels of ability. Equally, capacity and capability must be carefully judged so that they themselves or their followers are not in danger of "burn out."

Developing leaders

The management and transactional leadership of activities and human resources then goes much further than achieving corporate targets. The development of followers is important for their own levels of satisfaction but in a causal loop of positive pushes, the drive for success must also provide future leaders at all its levels. So, as well as judging the levels of work to provide stimulation, careful consideration should be made to the provision of rounded skills which produce future leaders from within. This not only involves careful talent selection, management, and retention of the potential individuals but also a control of the leader's own capability or a comfortable conscience of their own position. This is about letting go of one's own ego as much as holding on to good talent and letting it have the space it needs. It is not about measurement and control, which clips willing wings, but about proudly pushing forward talent from others and still labeling it as their talent not one's own. The greatness comes from the grooming of others not the snatching of their ideas or claustrophobic control of their energies.

This takes us back round to transformational territory and creates a different level of staying power for the organization, the leader, and the individuals within it.

Each side of the great leader above has a chapter devoted to it in this book. The purpose of each chapter is to explore the depth and directions of each side supported by quotes and short case parodies. It is hoped to stimulate creative and lateral thinking in the reader rather than preach a set of inflexible rules. The spirit of the text is less about academic definition and much more about a fission where selections of particular behaviors are indeed chosen and fused to form the most suitable leadership mix for each changing occasion.

Each side can stand on its own. Each side can blend with one or two others to form an appropriate hybrid. Each side links in cycle with the next one in the given model. All sides used together create synergy and make up THE GREAT LEADER.

CHAPTER 1

Being great

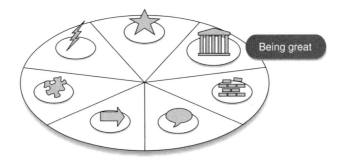

Being great

Source: Authors

Chapter introduction

What element within the leader is key to them being great? This is investigated through

Sense of timing

Knowing when to act as well as being in the right place at the right time

Sense of feeling for people

Understanding others and having an empathy with their position and perspective of the vision.

Sense of language levels

Being able to communicate at all levels in languages suitable for the situation

Transforming transactions to transcendence

Taking the tasks and lining them up with the overall cause in a spirit where staff want to do them rather than have to

Sense of presence

Being visibly in command with the right level of authority and approachability

Sense of self

Having confidence in self and a personal purpose which fits with that of the staff and the company

The paradoxical portfolio of alchemy

Bringing it all together in the right combinations

The elements which make up great leadership have been in question for millennia. Great figureheads have regularly emerged through this time and their character or image iconized as a good example of how leadership should be done. Not necessarily because we agree with them but certainly because we remember them.

From Socratic spiritual solution encouraged through independent and open thought in ancient Greece to Mao-esque dictator-driven order in recent East there has been no shortage of such memorable front liners to choose from.

From Sun Tzu's artful military master plans in ancient East to General Patton's visioning in recent West during WWII there has been no shortage of memorable method to peruse on.

Such greatness is as diverse as it is astounding and while it may be possible to cosmetically imitate a particular figure head or method, it is far more difficult to isolate and truly replicate the "great" component which actually made it all work successfully in the first place.

Whether great leadership starts with the individual, or lies with their followers, or hides in the organizational environment, or sits behind a particular method used is unclear. Therefore the "great rate" is volatile and can fluctuate according to a wide set of circumstances. A higher "great rate" must be achieved by considering the impact of decisions on all of these areas and so developing a contingency approach which chameleons itself to the situation. However, to be in the position of "contingent chameleon" the potentially great leader needs a portfolio of different methods to choose from. It is not just what they choose to use but how they use it, who they use it on, when they use it, and perhaps even where they take it, and now we are getting closer to seeing how difficult it is to be great.

The responsibility for the leader is huge and how much luck rather than judgment is involved with such an exercise of choice? It would be fair to say that strategic choice, direction, and implementation can be a bit of a lottery. Educated choices can be made using scientific data and projections but accuracy is in question when there is some chance involved. Is a great leader a great person in an ordinary situation or is a great leader an ordinary person in a great situation? Surely, great leaders would be able to make a silk purse from a sow's ear or turn base metal into gold. Being great must involve a Midas touch in ordinary circumstances, so *alchemy* rules. Of course, the cynical would suggest that being in the right place at the right time would count for a proportion of greatness which exists. A great situation might bring out the best in a perfectly ordinary figure. Do all leaders have the same chemical ingredients for greatness but only some have the potential and ability for *alchemy*? There may be a genetic or emotional something which separates the great from the ordinary. Perhaps an ability to see things that others can't or an instinct for what may be right. We cannot have it all, otherwise we would all be great or rather great would be the ordinary norm – so something special must exist.

Changing situations though – surely bring context into the equation for the leader rather than the hint of merely being born with the greatness. Context affects contingency choice. Situation styles the starting point. Context drives transactional need. Leaders control transactions and gear them toward, or transform them, into the vision ahead. Leaders also take full responsibility for their discretionary choice and the processes to bring the vision about. " ... as an executive generally you are held responsible for what management does ... ."

Case study comment

A chairman's model and message – The buck stops here!

" ... it is really the consultation on the interface between management and the board with clear delegations to management and clear accountability of management to the board and an overall responsibility of the board, both in terms of controlling the accountability and deciding more on things the company should know. The other side in terms of the accountability, becomes more complicated, as an executive generally you are held responsible for what management does and that is the model on which I presently operate."
Viscount Davignon

(One of the founders of the European Union)

" ... the interface between management and the board with clear delegations to management and clear accountability of management to the board and an overall responsibility of the board," has to thread right through the business. Understanding the day-to-day needs of the business is important. On a bottom up basis, a start with the front-line needs of the organization is a good foot hold for the front-line person of that business. The daily jobs, transactions, and tasks which turn the organization over are a key foothold to overall success. How each transaction contributes to the overall picture is an important consideration when beginning to lead followers forward in the right direction. Transactional leadership is that ability to cope with and control the daily operational tasks. It is activity driven and short term. The focus is on the execution of the transactions in the short term. Or is it? It could just be the ability to translate the day-to-day operational needs from the overall strategic vision to ensure that vision comes about. Once the transactional needs of the organization are decided, then the followers along with the tasks are led or rather managed on a more "micro" basis to transport all in the right direction. Indeed transactional leadership could be management in disguise which brings up the further point as to whether management is a part of leadership, leadership a part of management, and whether being a great leader is a balance or mixture of the two. A journey through the seven sides of great leaders will help bring forth the answer.

Walk the talk

Get out there and identify ten operational tasks in your business or service. Examine whether they are being conducted in an autonomous way particular to that department or function, and assess their contribution to the overall direction and vision of the company.

Now work it the other way. Start at the Vision end of the equation and break down to the same ten tasks. Have you a match or is there a gap for you to repair? Sort it out now.

More than this the vision is turned into a reality by breaking it down into manageable or "managed" parts and winning over the followers to do what is needed willingly. Transformational leadership gains that willing following with the transactions in mind to achieve the goals. Transformational approach is about getting staff to work with you because they want to – not for you and not because they have to. In addition to this there should be an understanding of how they work together, " ... blending people together..." in their teams and environment. This takes time and patience – "patience is important ... ."

Case study comment

Take time to bring teams together

"... so blending people together requires patience because you have to understand where the proper balance is and so patience is important."
Viscount Davignon

(One of the founders of the European Union)

So, is being great about personal character or choice of method? Are leaders born great or made great? What qualities actually make up the great leader? The answer is that there may be no one answer and that many things factor in the make up of being great.

When browsing across the range of great leaders in history it is nigh on impossible to compile a list of qualities which are common to all. The characteristics which make a leader great are not clustered or themed. The Churchillian characteristics which were "great" during wartime were certainly less than appreciated afterwards. This tells us that one way of leadership methods and abilities are not constant but ever changing. This tells us that you can be the flavor of the month one minute and quite out of fashion the next. This tells us that leaders – however great – are disposable and dispensable.

This chapter will not offer a magical equation or combination of traits for being great which will transfer to changing fashions and events. It will, however, open the reader's eyes to a number of factors for consideration toward achieving success and effectiveness. In context, this chapter starts off a self-searching, elliptical journey through different aspects of greatness which can be utilized at different levels and in different quantities. It helps the leader search for the right combination of skills for varying situations and so increases the likelihood of greatness from them. This audit and *alchemy* is also influenced by their ability to apply the right skills mix at the right time and their ability to apply the right skills mix appropriately to their staff, which requires feeling, *perception*, and empathy.

Sense of timing

What makes a leader great in one situation could make them incompetent in another and the increasing pace of change in today's business environment means then that different qualities will not only be needed at different times but also more quickly and drastically. Perhaps then, it is the ability to provide the appropriate leadership qualities and skills at the appropriate time that is the secret to being great. Perhaps, it is the ability to switch from the transactional needs of the business to the transformational thinking which links the followers toward the future which is key to successful timing.

It would then be necessary to be able to predict the right time to change approach and whether this is the science of transactional tactics or the art of transformational targeting is debatable. The day-to-day management information or an environmental analysis might give a scientific base on which to work and assess trends but also the "feeling" or intuition element of leadership gives rise to the need for an emotional level of intelligence and *perception*, not just of others but of self and of company. "Have you made yourself familiar with the key markets in which your company is acting? What are the trends? What are the competitors, and so on?" asks Dr. Bernd Scheifele, Chairman of the Managing Board, HeidelbergCement.

So what we are saying is that the sense of timing is loaded with qualitative and quantitative data and these are used to reduce risk and so increase the chance of greatness. This balance of statistical information with some intuitive foresight feeds the leader's decision in terms of *when* to act.

Walk the talk

Collate your management information and look at it afresh. Balance it with an honest overall environmental analysis of your business or service – that is, look at what does and will affect your sector in the next few years hence. Yes, we know you know how to do it but do you actually do this as often as you should?

Also backtrack the management information several years to isolate the trend to date and assess whether it does actually follow the path of the overall direction.

Case study comment

Know your facts

"... it is amazing to see how many people are sitting on supervisory boards and acting in an unreliable, irresponsible way because they do not care, they do not know the business, they just sit there, they approve things which they have not understood and if you would make a survey on the supervisory board members of the top 30 companies in Germany and would ask them one very simple question, 'when have you personally visited the biggest manufacturing site of the company where you are sitting on the board, when have you last discussed with the plant manager his problems? Are you familiar with the key success processes of your company? Have you made yourself familiar with the key markets in which your company is acting? What are the trends? What are the competitors, and so on?' If you would ask that question to these guys, 90% the answer would be 'No'. They have never been visiting a thing, they have never been discussing what is this? That's the key and that's also the problem in Germany now ... "

Dr. Bernd Scheifele – Chairman of the Managing Board, HeidelbergCement

Sense of feeling for people

Empathy with the follower is then also another component of being great. Being able to understand their needs or feelings and talk in their language ranges from translating long-term plans to short-term goals which motivate and inspire to gaining their feedback in an environment where they trust their future with you. Indeed, their feedback may even have an impact on the leader's decision for timing too. Given the great differences in individuals in terms of *perception* and ability, things become even more convoluted and complicated as this now requires the leader to be everything to all.

The importance of interpreting not only the vision or direction ahead but also the needs and feelings of the followers and the changing nature of the environment is high on the agenda of the great leader. Insight is as important as foresight and this is further assisted by a good working knowledge of those who work with us and for us. The leader can interpret behaviors and feelings more accurately from a firm foothold of cumulative data and deduct *how* to act.

Sense of language levels

If part of the key to success is ensuring followers believe in what they do and that what they do is geared toward the overall vision, then to transform the workforce, the leader must also be able to translate the overall vision into meaningful language to them. This is not just about relaying and evangelizing the cause, this is about talking the language of the follower at whatever level they exist. Leaders at translational level hold great power and responsibility. How something is relayed is key to the ultimate acceptance or rejection of it. Believing in a vision oneself is not enough, it needs to be understood and believed in at all levels and this requires careful and considered interpretation.

Language must be used which is appropriate to the audience to win them toward the overall goal. Interpretation is not just about language but also about task typing and division. The translation of the overall purpose into smaller purposes at different levels is as important as the translation of the overall purpose in the right language to all. The communication of how everything intertwines with everything else is an important part of achieving a true understanding and *followership*. This equally applies to the conduct of the leader themselves in terms of how they set an example. "...people are always watching you..." (Dr. Bernd Scheifele, Chairman of the Managing Board, HeidelbergCement)

Case study comment

Set the example

"I think you set the standards and if you ask for hard work, you had better make sure you work also very hard because otherwise people won't follow you. This sounds very simple but it is not that easy, because people are always watching you, so you have to be very careful in what you are doing. One principle should be that you should only do things which would not expose you if they were published in the media the next day. That is how you should behave."

Dr. Bernd Scheifele, Chairman of the Managing Board, HeidelbergCement

---

This good advice as regards leadership conduct is important as staff emulate the actions and attitudes of the leader and respect from the followership is gained through the communication of their behavior.

Of course, translation quality and loyalty to the company is also dependent on how the leader interprets events. Less than great leaders can make the mistake here of interpreting things for their own end and not for that of the organization. Their short-term gain can obstruct long-term company need should interpretation be less than worthy of the overall vision and more reliant on a personal goal.

Walk the talk

Collect or devise a hierarchical tree of all your staff including cleaners, security staff, receptionists, and so on. Put all of

▶

their names down in black and white. If you don't know them – find them out. Now also put down the last time you had a proper talk to them. Target a proper chat with all of them over the next few months with the objective of researching that what they do is geared toward the overall vision. Make a point of appreciating them and pointing out how their efforts help you and the overall cause.

Think carefully about the role of each staff member and work out in your head how their day or job pans out. Think ahead about what you think they need to know to help them understand your decisions and the direction of the company. Translate the overall vision in your head to activities and terminology each staff member will personally appreciate in their different roles.

Transforming transactions to transcendence

Transformational leadership has long been the opposite partner of transactional leadership. The essence of transformation is in the driving of the workforce toward the overall goal. This is less about the vehicle to deliver the right tasks and more about securing reality from the original intentions of the vision. The leader secures the willing and able following of the workforce so inspiring the way forward. More than this though, there is an enthusiastic introduction of ideas and change and thus emotional targets are set rather than the scientific ones of the transactional levels.

The satisfaction of completing something in the short term is now canopied by the knowledge of where it is going and the long-term landing of the task. Meaning to the work is evident and teams pulled together by purpose because there is a unified focus on vision. The cooperation of teams who are led transformationally is high as energy is channeled towards organizational goal and infighting less likely. Rather than compete with each other, individuals pull together to work against corporate competition.

Followers respect the personal nature and positive use of referent power where leaders use personality and humanness, and so followers work for the individual character at their head with respect rather than fear. Followers see where their job lies and how important it is to the organization so benefit in seeing a value to the completed task. This sense of value synergized with others not only creates a greater output but also the most correct output for the organizational vision as it is one which goes in the right direction.

Transcendent leadership has been offered as an alternative term for transformational leadership, but is it a type of, or a stage, or a component of, transformational leadership in its own right? It is described as the complete engagement of the emotional support of the followers and indeed that is what transformational leadership achieves. The followers believe in the way forward and work together toward it. To truly transcend though would mean that each individual really buys into the corporate goal/dream and truly becomes a part of it. It is not just a question of fellow workers, workers and superiors, or workers and organization being in tune and working together effectively. It is a true organizational *synergy* which creates something more than the components which make it up. A spiritual level of leadership is achieved and output goes beyond the range or limits expected. True transcendent leadership not only gets the existing team working to full potential but understands that this done well there is another level of being. "Extra" invisible followers are created from the **synergy** of the existing numbers and these outputs add to the force of success and so greatness.

A good leader can get four outputs from a team of four. The team will input anyway if adequately led. The poor leader will get less than four outputs from a team of four as the followers will divide and work against each other and the organization, and their energy becomes inwardly destructive rather than outwardly constructive. The great leader will get five or six outputs from a team of four. Having catered for their individual needs and tailored them and paralleled them with the corporate goals, they create an extra level of input and output which exceeds the sum of the individual parts. Not only are the existing four members of the team happier which creates a positive causal loop all round, the "extra" work by the invisible followers such *synergy* creates is free physical output which has organically grown from the positive emotional input of the team.

Transcendent leadership impregnates the vision deeply into each individual so that their own vision is exactly in line with it. This increases the chance of achieving the set vision as well as increasing the capacity of the existing resources by channeling emotional energy alongside physical energy.

In the same way and with the same spirit, daily, routine tasks must be monitored and controlled. How they are done, when they are done, who does them, how fast they are done, and where they are done are short-term matters for management consideration. Efficiency and cost control are key in helping the health of any business. Targets and budgets are there for a purpose. Keeping the machine running at core level is not just pure management of duty but a transactional leadership which values the building blocks which make up the whole. Each small transaction may mean little on its own, and indeed if mismanaged or misled, may wander off in the wrong direction. Pulled together and worked together, clusters of appropriate transactions develop a *synergy* which augments the whole.

Management has been much maligned in recent years. It has been as if it is a lesser skill when compared to the evolving and ever-fashionable leadership skills promoted by many writers. Such controls were seen as separate to and lesser than the driving inspiration of leadership.

The transactional leadership as defined in yesteryear referred to such management but brought it in as part of a leadership package and so acknowledged the importance of keeping the cogs of the wheel turning in the overall leadership picture. Today's transactional leadership is so much more than even that well-meant move. Management has recovered its secondary position and risen to partner leadership with strength. It is no longer just about the daily tasks which contribute to the overall picture but about a deliberate and transformational choice of particular transactions based on that vision. Part of the great leader's role is to carefully choose the transactions as well as monitor them. The tasks are handpicked to complement and transform the direction of the organization and then controlled and monitored to ensure that they are completed in the intended way.

Equally, it is not just the contribution that this makes to the overall which is key to greatness but the attention to particular motivation at the different levels to maximize output. Each transaction then is truly led rather than simply controlled and staff are inspired and transformed at all levels in the company. Transactional leadership therefore is woven throughout the organization and part of a cycle of greatness. Managing meaningfulness into the process of transaction is indeed transformational in nature.

Whether such leadership comes from one particular individual as part of a team which make up the greatness or whether one individual has the capacity to do this along with the other types of leadership is up for debate.

What matters is that the job gets done. No – correction – what matters is that the right job gets done well and in line with organizational requirement and vision. "...the fundamental roads along which this organisation is or ought to be traveling." (Vanni Treves, Chairman of Korn Ferry International). Transactional leadership is a part of, and is fed by, transformational leadership and therefore an important part of being great.

Case study comment

Line up tactics with strategy

"You then, it seems to me, have to concentrate on what the strategies of the company are or should be. Now strategy is a big word, it can be used very loosely. I use it with great care. But nevertheless you have to try to cut away what it is

▶

> that makes the organisation function on a daily basis, and say, standing back as best one can, what are the directions, the crucial directions, the fundamental roads along which this organisation is or ought to be travelling. So, the Board needs to have a pretty clear sense on where it is that this organisation is or ought to be going. Some of the things that the company is doing might be things that it ought not to be doing because they have no future. If that is the conclusion, how do we get rid of them? Some of the things the company is doing, some of the businesses it is in show exceptional promise, help them maximise that. That kind of overview of the company's strategic goals and aspirations as distinct from the business as usual environment you have to deal with that as well but it is separable."
>
> Vanni Treves, Chairman of Korn Ferry International (UK)

Having traveled from transaction to transcendence, a light can be shed on the quality of great leadership. Perhaps it starts with a high level of ability to inspire others through evangelization. Setting out and crafting the future and communicating it with great energy and passion to all. It would follow then that once this is orated from on high and followers clear of the long-term direction that the transformation is in progress. The vision once evangelized needs to be translated into manageable parts and day-to-day language. Then the transactions undertaken with a sense of purpose and meaning are transported in the right direction. Teams are encouraged to work together and truly transform the organization.

This transformational aspect could be down to character or communicative ability. It could be what we see in a leader which makes us follow or it could be what we hear. It could be both.

Greatness must lie within the individual to begin with and as many singers can sing but only a few have the "X" factor, then many a leader can lead adequately but only some have the "great" or "Xtra" factor.

Sense of presence

The attractiveness, appealability, and charm of a leader grow from using qualities they have from within. These internal qualities or *charisma* inspire the *followership* to listen and understand, and this commences the transformation process of best use, motivation, and encouragement of their cooperation, participation, and full integration in the way forward. The innate characteristics of the leader make up this appeal and they themselves become a symbol, even a brand, of the company. The image they portray and what they say as well as how they say it becomes pivotal to their persuasive strength. The power of their passion and its alignment with corporate cause will be a key factor here also. This is the transformational part of being great as opposed to merely controlling or dictating a situation which most or many ordinary leaders could do anyway. The attractiveness, magnetism, and sense of passion for the cause itself attracts a further layer of willing input from followers which may not ordinarily have been achieved. The attractiveness thus extracts the "Xtra" factor from the workforce and so achieves the *synergy* the ordinary leader cannot.

On the subject of attractiveness, it is interesting for a moment to swing back on the usual meaning of the word. In addition to the character elements suggested here as attractive, followers may be swayed by the physical look of the leader too. If so, the degree to which this occurs would be interesting to note particularly in this televisual age.

Politics like many things today have become subject to the visual vote. Seismic judgment is suddenly made in split seconds based on how contenders look and this comes ahead of what they know and who they are. These cosmetics contribute to that "Xtra" factor with their opposites or worse blandness and even sometimes baldness awarding a perfectly good candidate the "Xit" factor and a way out of the competition.

Notably, this is subject to follower or organizational need. Perhaps it is the follower who really defines the charisma/character of the leader they want. In selection they have their shopping list for the right elements for that time and place. Greatness is and will be defined and awarded by followers rather than the other way round.

If greatness is decided and attributed by the follower then subordination is voluntary or at least manipulated. Greatness is then defined not only by an **"X" factor** within but also an "Xternal" factor without. That enthusiastic *followership* validates the great characteristics and so encourages more of them or improvement of them. This makes the great leader greater or perhaps it makes the ordinary leader extraordinary. No, followers are not fools. The leader must have that special something to start with. It may then grow from there but a greatness must be there to work with or at least something which is appealing to them and just to complicate matters further, this too can vary considerably.

Studies during the BT Global Challenge on the leadership traits of the yacht captains showed that all podium winners display a particular characteristic which would not instantly be held or known as "great". Interestingly, all scored high on the *"vulnerability"* score. This showed that they were human, they showed not only their commitment to the cause and their competence to achieve but also that they were also subject to error, not perfect and indeed needed their followers – they could not do it on their own. This apparent weakness must increase their likeability factor and bring them closer to their *followership* and indeed become a strength.

This introduces the thought that *humility* could be a factor in greatness. Sensing the level of self to put forward may contribute to greatness.

Sense of self – Narcissism

Along with character or charisma there must be an element of *narcissism*, or love for self, in those who put themselves forward for such leadership positions. A great leader must want to get on and have a need to be liked to volunteer to go under such volatile view. That personal strength of personality is also attractive to the follower who needs to know that their leader can actually hack it.

What is clear from this is that what those great elements actually are in the first place will never be precisely defined. The different needs of the followers at any given time and the different needs of the organization during changing times mean greatness is as is appropriate to the situation.

Situational leadership studies turn attention away from searching for traits in individuals and incorporate the types of reaction or behavior the leader displays in different circumstances. Some examine different levels of consultation and participation with followers. Some acknowledge the level of ability and willingness of the followers. Some view the balance between focus for profit and focus for people. They suggest and define a particular default to a leadership style. The leader naturally falls within a certain character profile so that they are pigeon holed by behavioral trait rather than character trait.

Such personal evaluation questionnaires serve well to initiate the investigative process on how to improve or make greater the natural leadership styles but can also be limiting in that they categorize leaders in a finite way rather than encourage the rounded approach of accruing many of the great skills needed.

If we all do default to a particular set of behavioral traits then does that mean it is then indeed the situation or the *followership* which decides the level of greatness or great rate of the time? If this is the case then does that limit our ability to act in all situations – are we only suitable for certain ones in Churchillian manner or can we change and make ourselves greater? By accruing skills which do not necessarily come naturally to us and adding them to the ones we are born with we can make ourselves great leaders. Perhaps there is something in widening our portfolio of skills in order we are indeed more appropriate for more situations. With a wider range of abilities we are more likely to become the *contingent chameleons* ready to survive in a wider range of situations.

Walk the talk

Why do your followers follow you and keep you in your current position? What is it about you they like? Is there anything you think they may not like? Is there anything you can do to your manner or even appearance to make yourself more approachable to them?

Now a very tricky one – what do you think your shelf life is in this role? How could you extend it?

The paradoxical portfolio of alchemy

The logical and chemical make up of being great still avoids exact definition. The base metals to work with vary considerably and turning them into gold to achieve metaphorical *alchemy* involves a wide range of processes. The great leader follows no particular recipe for success to exact proportion. Judgment and discretion in partnership with *perception* and *flexibility* increase the chances of adding the right things to the pot at the right time so the right mix results for the situation at hand.

Being great, rather than ordinary, therefore requires the leader to swing from one place to another quickly and therefore deal with *paradox*. Investment in increasing or sharpening the skills on the shelf of leadership greatness is necessary so that they can be used appropriately at the right time. Having this shelf of skills from which to draw will inevitably extend the shelf life of their leadership in the organization as well as truly transform the business.

Organizations have classically changed their leaders regularly as particular "great trait" clusters go out of fashion with economic, social, or technological change. The average shelf life of the CEO cannot be much more than several years. It has been a habit to indulge in change for a new model of greatness when appropriate to circumstances for some time. How long this can continue without adverse effect is questionable and there is good ground for thinking that an ever-improving continuum of greatness is more likely to be born from increasing the abilities of the leaders to change with the change itself.

This is not to say that all leaders could last forever and indeed each leader will have a certain shelf life but extending their "great date" may have exceptional benefits to the company. Retaining the experience for that bit longer will mean that more personal and pertinent decision making is likely. Their being in line with the organization and flexible to it is key. "What is the embodiment of the organisation, what has made it function well or badly in the period before I took Office?" asks Vanni Treves, Chairman of Korn Ferry International.

Case study comment

Line up yourself with the organization

"The first thing I do is try to understand what the principles, if you like, of the organisation are. What is the embodiment of the organisation, what has made it function well or badly in the period before I took Office? And, in particular, what are the motivations, the drivers of the senior people there. What are their aspirations, not only for themselves of course, but for the corporate being for which they work. I do not believe that the behaviour of a Chairman or a leadership team can be imposed on an organisation irrespective of where that organisation has come from and how it has got to where it is."

Vanni Treves, Chairman of Korn Ferry International (UK)

The "great rate" of the future leader will be determined by their ability to adjust to situational challenge speedily and appropriately to ensure their organization is in a "great state". In addition to being graded by what is within the leader in terms of character and a portfolio of different skills and then how they use them accordingly, follower sophistication will also change and increase in line. As followers become even more aware of what they want and need and what the organization wants and needs, they will have more and more of a say in not only the choice of leader but also the shelf life of the leader and also have a major impact on the strategic direction of the organization they work for.

If being great involves all the traits mentioned above, then it becomes evident that it is only the start of the equation of leadership success. The *followership* influence on that success is also affected by the degree of leader transformation and transaction, or perhaps the balance of both, which takes place between them and their followers.

By first discussing what is great in terms of particular characteristics, qualities or abilities, it is clear that a number of leadership personalities or "sides" emerge from this which may be used in cycle or as appropriate. "Being Great" is only the first of the seven sides of great leaders and thus represents a whole window to the leadership soul.

Conclusion

Being great is one of the seven sides of great leaders but as we travel through the six other sides we can also see it is the encompassment of those six sides too and therefore a whole mix of abilities at ground and creative level. Being great is one thing and all things.

Great rate

This chapter has touched on some of the elements of "being great." It is not a definitive list but the elements which seem to make the difference involve

Alchemy

Charisma

Contingent Chameleon

Ego

▶

Flexibility

Followership

Humility

Narcissism

Paradox

Perception

Synergy

Transforming

Vulnerability

X Factor

CHAPTER 2

Crafting the future

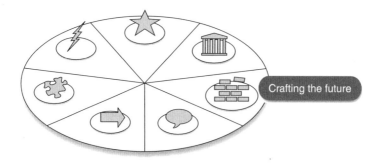

Source: Compiled by authors

Chapter introduction

Creating a future/destination and planning the journey there. Strategic and tactical targeting and selling to achieve the overall goal. This is viewed through

Vision and visioning

Defining the difference between the Vision which is the way forward and Visioning which is the art of getting there

Vision and mission

Understanding the difference between the direction of the organization and its purpose

The result of visioning lethargy

What happens when Visioning is not practiced properly?

▶

Power

Different types of power and how they can be used

The components and results of visioning success

Getting it right, what it takes, and how it affects the business

Linked to "being great," the leader must have the ability from within themselves to most effectively utilize the available physical and human resources and to create and set the vision for the organization at the same time. Inspiration and perspiration work together as the great leader ensures and indeed actually crafts the future so all have a clear and deliberate direction in which to travel. That direction is the same as that of the organization.

Determining the future to create the vision and craft the way forward is not left to guesswork. There must be a detailed and informed level of prediction which stems from scientific fact leading the decisions but of course also mixed with the fine art of risk in being able to "feel/know" the way forward which will be best for the organization. Deciding on the destination in the future takes courage and determination but the journey is as much part of crafting the future as is the future itself. Risk taking is therefore tempered by reality so the future is within sight and an achievable motivation as well as *destination determination*.

To get to that future a series of juggling acts will be necessary as conflicting interests from outside and in create natural hurdles. Competitor strength and direction will have its own influence on the direction chosen in terms of choices between investment driven paths and/or cost driven paths. Achieving or maintaining a competitive position in the marketplace is only the start. Both shareholder and customer push in on the leader for their own deal from the equation. Both can vote with their feet, both demand value and both must be kept satisfied they are getting it.

Walk the talk

Analyze how your competitors have influenced your strategic direction and design and write it out in a manner as if
explaining it to your front line staff. In the same manner
justify the path taken – for example, why differentiation
driven.

Sketch out a brief customer versus shareholder analysis by
evaluating the pros and cons for both from the answers
above.

However, well thought out, however beautifully balanced and
however well scientifically supported, the journey forward will
still involve significant change which will take the internal
customers that is, the staff, providing the products, services,
functions etc. well outside of their personal comfort zones. In
transforming the organization to achieve the future set and balance all interested parties, some *transmutation* must take place.
This essentially means lining up the old practices and beliefs
with the new. Merging these practices then needs very careful
thought and planning in itself.

Thus, the great leader not only creates the future in deciding
what it is in the first place but also crafts the future in making the
overall vision a daily, manageable prospect. People and processes at all levels of the business must be in tune with the corporate song. In addition to maintaining an excitement and passion
for the chosen future for the whole workforce to get caught up in
and enjoy, deliberate direction must be drilled in all departments
and divisions so all of the daily duties which contribute to the
overall picture are driven toward the destination. This is not simply ensuring that each tactical task is directly linked to the vision,
but a considered and careful evolution of current practice retaining old strengths and developing new ones fit for the future.

The pertinent use of power to make things happen, the securing
of shareholder dividend and the choosing of the channel leading
to competitive advantage to court the customer to spend, all

provide the mix for success. This mix creates a further power which must be maintained and sustained and also able to halt itself to check any digressions when splits in *visioning* arise – as they inevitably will – however good the leader.

So vision is the creation of the future, not the crafting of it. The crafting of the future is the set of subelements carefully calculated to ensure that vision actually happens. Such tailoring needs a great leader to offer clear communication channels in all directions which means that translating the vision and the subparts of the vision thereof is an essential part of the process. It is not enough to rely on a personal conviction to the created vision and relay that to the staff, it is absolutely necessary to link all parts of the organization with the right levels of communication. From *conductor to conduit*, the great leader does more than direct the performance; they hold together and actually connect and oxygenate all parts of the business.

Competent communication is not just about cascade but also collection. As well as evangelizing all that is good about the future in a top down fashion, effective leaders cultivate a culture of cooperation and so ensure a feedback culture channels communications from the bottom up. This can only benefit Board level decision making as real time quantitative fact and up-to-the-minute qualitative opinion make the right decisions more likely. When asked about her leadership style Baroness Maggie Jones, the renowned social activist who help senior ranks in UNISON the large trade union, gives honest account of a rounded approach which cultivates such cooperation.

Case study comment

Charismatic cooperation

"I think I'm inclusive; I think I'm good at listening; I think I'm good at drawing out key points from a debate and good at structuring a debate; I'm making it clear how a debate

▶

was going to be conducted so everybody knows where they are so I can explain things clearly to people; a certain warmth about the way that I chair things that people relate to; I'm respectful of people when they have a contribution to make that I couldn't possibly know about so I certainly don't tend to try and impress people with a knowledge that I don't have. So I think you've got to be open about what you do know and what you don't know. I think its ordinary intelligence and common sense really."

Baroness Maggie Jones, House of Lords, ex-Unison

Vision and visioning

Vision is leadership destination. Or perhaps it would be more accurate to define vision as organizational destination rather than have it as the egoistical arrival point of the CEO. It is the product of foresight and the projected image of the organization although it would be an interesting study to ascertain how many destinations are corporate led rather than individual led. Not all leaders have the interests of the organization as a priority and their own survival may come far into their decision making equations.

Presuming the great leader has organizational welfare as the priority they can not only create the future by looking forward, they can also foresee events and indeed avoid catastrophes. This calculated and educated *vision* though is the end point and a full *visioning* commitment involves not only the whole strategic direction but also the tactical planning processes to support it. This process of *visioning* crafts that future and proactively moulds it to shape the future chosen.

The key themes which emerge then are, the level of the leader's individual and personal commitment to the vision or at least the acting ability to look like they are, the persistent relaying of the key values of that vision throughout the process and finally making sure it is communicated in the appropriate way for the levels involved. "So I think that feeling a strong empathy and a very, very powerful desire to identify with, what you understand to be the goals or the mission of the organization, is absolutely fundamental." (Lord Tom Sawyer, Member of the House of Lords and ex-Chairman of The Notting Hill Housing Trust).

Successful visionary leadership creates the end future goal and crafts how to get there. It also gives the organization, the teams and each individual their own reason for going there. Each individual should get their own personal value out of the whole *visioning* process as an equal objective to having them buy into the key values of that vision.

Walk the talk

Up close and personal! Take time out to privately plot your own vision for your own future. Now match it to that of the company and your followers. Be truthful to yourself – are you going in the same direction or are you constantly in internal conflict.

Case study comment

"I think the most important thing is that you've got to feel really passionate about the organisation that you've been invited to chair or that you stand to chair. I've got my passions in life that will motivate me to try and achieve excellence. I wouldn't achieve excellence in an organisation that I didn't perhaps enjoy empathy. So I think that feeling a strong empathy and a very very powerful desire to identify with, what you understand to be the goals or the mission of the organization, is absolutely fundamental.

I'm very value driven, I like to think that what I'm doing is of value to the people that I'm doing it for, I think that's more important to me than anything, wanting to give

▶

something to a community or to an organisation that they value. I've never really been driven by money, money is nice it pays the bills but I never felt that it was something that was hugely important to me. I've always been more interested in do I identify with the values of the organisation."

Lord Tom Sawyer, House of Lords and ex-Chairman of The Notting Hill Housing Trust.

Such creative transformation and indeed *transmutation* is convoluted and requires a good level of emotional intelligence. There is a need to understand the emotional needs of the workforce as well as the practical activities and tasks required to arrive at the goal.

Then, even above that there is more. Keeping abreast of the markets, understanding and predicting trends for the future is essential. One eye on the inside of the business penetrating every level is important but so is the other eye on the outside seeing ahead – again at every level and angle. Being able to read the terrain and plan is one thing but being able to brief the middle tank commander to scale and seize it, is quite another. Equally, gaining competitive territory is fine as long as customer value is maintained to standards worthy of repeat business and visits. How this then weighs up with shareholder investment is difficult. Cost competition has to be considered by most at some time or other but literally at what price. Leaner margins for larger market share may mean less lucrative investment. The battle toward achieving the vision never really ends.

Vision and mission

Vision is direction and ultimate destination so what is mission and where does it sit in terms of crafting the future? Most organizations have a Vision and also a Mission statement which gives a sense of their future direction. Differentiating the two can sometimes be difficult. Mission is meaning, purpose and identity. Direction and meaning work together and the whole process of *visioning* encompasses both.

An organization without a clear vision or the direction and purpose of a considered *visioning* process is likely to have its energies turned inwards. "I think that has input from all parts of the organization..." says Val Gooding, CEO of BUPA, Britain's largest private health insurance company, on the responsibility for vision. If everyone is not journeying in the same direction for the long term and strengthening for and against change, then a weaker institution will result and the organization is left in the past.

Case study comment

"the CEO has to articulate the vision and has to be inspiring when articulating it but how it gets distilled into a motivating statement for an organisation, I don't think that is just the CEO. I think that has input from all parts of the organisation, possibly from the board, possibly from the stakeholders, shareholders, or customers, or employees or others, and I think the model/idea of a CEO who sits with a wet towel around their head for their first 100 days, then emerges with a new vision for the organisation, is very old fashioned these days. I just don't think that is realistic. I think people who do that are at quite a big risk of being too remote from what is actually happening with their market, their stakeholders and then maybe coming out with a vision that actually doesn't inspire anybody and everyone thinks, 'my God, she's mad, what has happened now?'"

Val Gooding, CEO of BUPA

The result of visioning lethargy

Chaos

Without a clear long-term direction the organization evolves in many directions. Not only is the direction divided but the purpose or mission also becomes divided and it is not long before these conflict with the organizational goals themselves or indeed each other.

Rather than using corporate energy to strengthen competitive standing in the organization's business environment, energy is used to fight each other and duplication of effort occurs.

These splits of vision through the working ranks have serious consequences and are worsened if also evident at Director level. This results in chaos being cascaded from above as well as accumulated from within and the internal competition which subsequently results from that ensures a declining performance as well as a declining respect for the organization from its inhabitants as they guard their own skins and use all their energy to survive. Such a vicious spiral promotes accelerated attrition with the exiting staff able to strengthen competitors instead of the originating organization itself.

Walk the talk

Analyze the staff turnover figures for the last several years. How do they compare with industry norms? Of the staff who have left – are there any you feel you should have retained?

Split ranks

As a result of internal division or indeed as a cause of it, the organization without its future crafted will have split ranks at the higher levels. These split ranks in authority then essentially create and craft their own different futures so the organization actually becomes several organizations which compete with each other. Not only is internal competition of a negative nature grown but also confusions occur as loyalties become divided and mixed. Without just the one overall vision to believe in and strive toward, the staff become torn as to where to give their support and may find the political power games too much. Contradiction and conflict replaces hope and motivation and staff find their input meaningless so they reduce their output and also hold off their precious and informative input to the decision making process. They are also likely to develop a personal agenda to work to, one which protects themselves and their teams, so a lack of alignment occurs between the individual and the desired future of the organization.

The negative autonomy makes a vicious spiral through the hierarchies of the organization and a collection of small companies essentially eat away at the healthy structure of the whole. The weakened entity cannot make as much progress in its external competitive environment and as if that was not punishment enough for not having a crafted future, a culture of in fighting becomes established and is very hard to shift once in.

Internal warfare

In the confusion within the company the competing directions do more than merely contradict each other. Personnel power encircles its cause to create and craft its own purpose, albeit in a smaller and internal environment. All energies now go into proving the choice they have each individually made is the right one and all respect for different opinions subsides. Colleagues become enemies and the internal support structures of the organization become battlegrounds for point proving and power struggles. Each separate cause pulls back progress from any other cause and the sabotage makes the gaining of any external competitive ground impossible.

Such an environment and attitude is infectious and self-perpetuating. Existing staff will exhaust themselves and inevitably look elsewhere for inspiration and motivation. New staff joining the organization walk straight into the discontent and also are less likely to commit. The high attrition is also high in cost as recruitment and training budgets burst and the company works very hard just to stay put in the present.

Such a "present held position" means procedures and processes change gear accordingly and staff look less far ahead – just to cope.

Walk the talk

Evaluate past and present conflict in your workplace. Consider how departments/functions could be brought closer together where conflict has occurred. Investigate why the conflict happened and produce a solution to prevent its recurrence.

Myopia

Survivalist coping mechanisms are now in place and the myopic demeanor of the individual getting through their working day becomes the norm. The organization is now on a sand bed of many agendas and its own future has shrunk further back too. With a weakened market position, the organization has no choice but to start thinking shorter term itself and is in need of faster results. These results become further removed from the vision and purpose of the company and more tailored to saving itself by more desperate measures. Future planning, never mind, crafting, is abandoned for fast gain and this further weakens the long-term ability of the company. Short-term goals are set and then reset creating and crafting a ground hog day where a repetition treadmill redirects effort the wrong way, again and again. The short-term goals need positioning in a long-term aim to become truly valuable.

Power

Much of the above relies on a misuse or misdirection of power. In general people in the same positions have the same power. The interesting thing is not actually the amount of power they have according to their position, but how they use it, or indeed, abuse it. Good use of *positional power* can pull staff in the right direction toward the corporate goal. Misuse of power, whatever type, can pull those staff in different directions. This can be deliberate and also accidental. Deliberate misuse of power will occur in the situations outlined above. Senior staff with their own agendas may use their power to serve their own ends, rather than that of the organization. Accidental misuse of power may occur when leaders do not realize how much they actually influence situations and are careless. Therefore, it is necessary to try and understand what power is and where it comes from. There is more to power than achieving transactional tasks.

Power used correctly can positively influence change and ensure followers do travel in the direction of the crafted out future. This then takes more than having the power, it takes a real understanding of the results of using it and misusing it. It is more than a possession from which to influence events, it is a complicated leadership lever in its own right. The power levers then need to be pulled appropriately according to situational context to ensure all parties are on the right track. This then makes the use of the power a transformational one which crafts the future and is used well in line with and not instead of power to drive transactional tasks or transmutate the business.

Whichever slant on power we have, it is an obvious ingredient in achieving vision and its use is also part of the *visioning* process. Power is used then through a set of levers to make things happen – short term and long term- and importantly in synchronization.

Levers for making things happen

Which lever to pull and when? – that is the question!

Isolating where the *power levers* exist is a good place to start for a new leader intending to be great or indeed an existing leader who wishes to be greater. Power exists at all levels of the business and can be subtle or obvious. It not only exudes from the holder but is influenced by others and the environment as well as available resources. Captured as a power flower at the end of this section (Figure 2.1) research isolates six critical power levers, positional power, personality power, particular power, perspective power, partnership power and professional power. The right power portfolio packs a hefty punch.

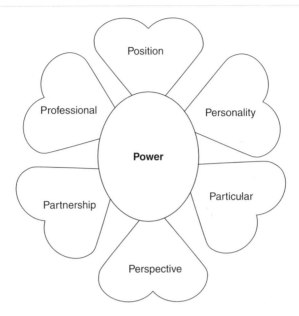

Figure 2.1   The power flower

Source: Compiled by authors

Positional power

By right of position we all have power. Whether we grab a clip board and strut around with a "New Manager Syndrome" because we are not yet used to how to wear it, is down to experience and indeed, in some cases, inclination. This power is authority by rank. So what does the great leader do with this power that is different?

Such position is a privilege and the power which accompanies it is a privilege. With the position comes responsibility for others, seeing to their individual and team needs, serving them and lining them up with long-term goals in a positive way. The great leader sees their role as a service to their staff as well as being a link to the overall cause and uses *positional power* to also position others in the direction of the vision and in a direction which also suits the follower.

This is *praising positional power* which positively pushes people toward the vision. Reward is used correctly to motivate followers in extrinsic and intrinsic fashion so they gain an individual value from the overall journey. Positioned in the right direction, they are more likely to perform the shorter-term tasks to target in this way.

Its nemesis is *punitive positional power* which negatively uses fear as its lever through coercion. This is not to say that some coercion is not needed from time to time. There will always be staff and situations which require it. Its use should be careful and sparing. Abused, this power can gain short-term results from the frightened followers who do the jobs because they have to and leave their real respect for the leader along the way. Demanded respect is worthless and encourages less cooperation in the long term as staff do only what is required of them and no more and indeed sometimes even sabotage the duties. This then has an effect on the overall picture in terms of delays, wrong outcomes, and so on.

Personality power

Attractiveness is power too. This is more than just a physical portfolio of factors which make someone nice to look at. It would be naïve to state that physical looks do not play a role in the way followers regard their leaders. Inevitably judgments are made on the way people look or appear and are key to what they buy into. Followers migrate toward attractiveness so image and character play a part in luring staff toward the end goal. This "pretty" power is not just about actually being pretty though. "Business Beauty" may have a place in the first impression but attractiveness must extend a longer term hook of other elements which appeal to the follower.

Admiration, reverence, adulation, and some level even of worship in some cases are not founded on good looks alone, although we should acknowledge they often help in the initial stages. However physically attractive a person is, it will then be their character/personality which wins through to gain the long lasting following of the troops.

This is quite difficult to define as it is a certain appeal, a certain charm that some leaders just seem to have. Some great leaders seem to have a magnetic and magical make-up which makes

them more memorable than others. Also, it is not always trans-
ferable. Beauty is in the eye of the beholder so what is attractive
to one set of followers may not be so to another.

This power lever of appealability is useful when dealing with staff,
and of course superiors, directly. It is an extra level of ammunition, if one has it, to use toward pulling staff toward the crafted
future although it should be stressed that it is not one which would
stand strong in its own right. Followers are too sophisticated to be
held by such cosmetics for very long. Other more sustainable
levers of power must be used alongside this one.

Equally, care should be taken in using attractiveness and adora-
tion. Many a leader spends a good deal of time making themselves attractive to their followers. Image consultants are well
rewarded in such a commercial age as this. It is possible to reach
a point where a great leader is so positively revered that the only
way is down. Reverence has its own shelf life as people change
and want something new. Fresh is only fresh for a while and
perhaps the great leader must keep crafting a future self which
fits with the crafting of the future of the organization to keep
their own shelf life as long as possible. The NIV (*New Improved
Version*) of the great leader themselves must also be a factor in
the *visioning* process.

Particular power

Along with the art of using position and personality wisely, the
great leader should have a healthy respect for the science and
power of management data. Management information and its
pedantic detail are vital in decision making and are as much of
creating and crafting the future as other levers available. The
devil may be in the detail in that problems will be spotted with
good management information sources which are properly analyzed. Also, destination, direction, and distribution of duties
will all have their numerical breakdown. Numbers and detail
justify the way forward as well as audit what is done.

Numbers are the business barometer. Leaders must know how
the business is actually doing at any given moment and also how

the different levels of the business are doing in terms of their contribution, or not, to it. This may seem obvious but it is not uncommon for leaders to become distracted by the overall cause and lose control of the quantitative qualifications necessary for internally supported success. In addition to keeping staff emotionally secure and happy in their work and directing them forward in the right way, it is also essential to ensure they have a job to be secure and happy in. However well liked a leader is, they will become far less respected if their basic business skills are not as strong as their people skills.

Ensuring the right management information is supplied is key. Careful analysis of this will reveal the correct decision making criteria for the business. The organizational activities will be evident in black and white and comparable to other factors in the business for prudent perusal. Reading the stats is a skill and it is as important to recognize what is *not* there as well as what is instantly evident.

Numbers power can be used positively and negatively in the same way as and perhaps as part of *positional power*. Some leaders can abuse the situation and deprive staff from number knowledge they need simply to pander to their own sense of importance. They can even cultivate a fear culture where the numbers are used on a "name and shame basis," "name and tame basis" or "name and blame basis," so effort is taken off performance for the company and becomes a matter of one's own survival. The translation of the overall numbers to the staff is also key. A leader can put their own personal translation before that of the organization and cause confusion or division in the ranks.

The great leader will use the numbers carefully and construc-tively. Staff will be informed of data on as open a basis as possible so they see where they fit into the overall picture and how each of their efforts affects the bottom line. Equally, the numbers may be used for open comparison in the organization, but more likely on a *"name and fame* basis" so participants are inspired and motivated by their presence and learn to respect the power of the numbers in their own right. The statistics are translated in terms of the corporate cause.

Corporate performance indicators cascade to the different levels of personal performance indicators for the individual and once everyone is using the same calculator a positive corporate sum evolves. Therefore, the moral of the story is – do the maths with a plus key!

Perspective power

Putting all of the aforementioned into context and leveling it all with the internal and external environment of the organization takes *power levers* to different levels. Not taking information or numbers in isolation but placing them in a fair context is also a particular power the great leader must acquire or refine. Greater degrees of accuracy result from more rounded approaches to decision making.

Even in terms of creating the future to begin with, the leader must understand where the organization is in terms of its competition and external environment in general. What market changes ahead will affect the running of the business may be dictated by economic trend, changing demographics, social trends and so on. It is this understanding which makes sure the right future is crafted in the first place or at least the risk is as calculated as possible.

Internally, the figures can be contextualized in many ways. New staff cannot directly be league tabled with experienced ones, new departments/stores/branches/services with old ones, and so on. A logical contextualization is necessary as is an emotional one. There also needs to be an ability to line up events with team dynamics, individual circumstances (within reason) and hierarchical relationships – things which do not show up on the management information figures but things which enormously affect them.

Partnership power

Networking is a strong power lever at any level of the business, but the great leader must set the pace and the example. More than the power to "nod and grin" at social events, this is clever and calculated contact building for the benefit of the business – using external parties although it could be said that used internally it is akin to *personality power*. Perhaps it is external *personality power*, persuasive power or party power.

To double play the term, one could turn party power inwards and state that it is *personality power* at another level – one which creates a fun environment for staff to work in and bonds teams together – a social power. Either way it is partnership, network, and relationship building. Collecting connections at all levels it is also a coalition power which internally and externally increases power levels and opportunities for the individual concerned and the business.

As with all power though, this too can be abused. Some relationships can become so successful in themselves that they start excluding other opportunities after a time. A club or niche mentality can form and the groupthink which results can be detrimental to progress and hold back the crafted future.

Professional power

Experience and expertise will always be respected by all levels so gaining and retaining it will always ensure a level of and indeed a lever of power. In depth knowledge of the business or a track record gained elsewhere brings with it a power currency which holds its rate well inside the company and out. Such hard currency also brings with it levels of confidence about the business and this type of power is more stand alone than the others in that its longevity makes it the most sustainable.

The difference in successful companies with one vision and great leadership is that corporate well-being is paramount and power and practices are geared toward corporate cause. Rather than fight over individual differences of leaders of the same level, value, manage and respect them, however they conflict with their own. Power struggles in the Boardroom stay there, they conduct themselves with the "Boardroom Handshake" and conflicts are not continued on the shop floor as such. This is done with the knowledge that such demonstrative power struggles could seriously hold back progress toward the crafted future.

Walk the talk

Using the "Power Flower" assess your particular strengths and weaknesses in power terms. Develop a simple action plan to refine the power skills you lack.

Baroness Maggie Jones, sports a penchant for a successful mix of powers in describing her time in UNISON, the very large "workers" union. Referring to the power flower model (Figure 2.1) her account shows the mix of perception, restriction, freedom, motivation as well as respect for the staff and their abilities.

Case study comment

Power flower at work

"Managing the department? I mean that was the first time that I started really to learn proper management skills in my own right. But, Unison was then a big organisation, you know, £100m+ turnover. This started having much more formal structured management systems quite rapidly. So we were moving towards trying to get 'Investors in People', we had proper training, assessments of staff, we had a much more formal, structured system. I think most people feel that I was successful in doing that. I ran, I think, a happy department. People liked being in the department. Not many people left. Lots of people stayed there. It was run on good management principles I would say, which is what you need to have for clear boundaries and clear guidelines

▶

of what is acceptable and what is not acceptable. But you also need to motivate people and take an interest in what they are doing. Give them clear advice, clear expectations, find new opportunities for them. A lot of it is about acknowledging and saying thank you when people do things well as well as noticing when things aren't so good. It takes a lot of time to do it well, but a lot of the staff in the department were graduates. They were high fliers in their own right. They didn't want me on their backs all the time nit picking about what they were doing. So, my management style was very much to give them their head but, you know, we had boundaries about what was acceptable and what wasn't acceptable and all the deadlines that had to be met."

Baroness Maggie Jones, House of Lords, ex-Unison.

The future crafted

The components of visioning success are personal passion, synchronized seniority, polylogue (multiple dialogue) and hypermetropia (long-sightedness).

Personal passion

Crafting the future is a risky process so it follows that the intensity of passion from the leader is seen at all times. This passion is obvious and useful at the beginning but must also have staying power as difficulties set in and the staff begin to question the goals. The great leader must truly believe in what they are preaching to the troops and not be seen to weaken. Internal dynamics and politics will test the levels on the journey forward so it is imperative the leader has their own internal belief correctly directed.

Synchronized seniority

It is all very well for the leader to be completely passionate about the crafted future, but this will be countered by confusion if the leader has not looked after the seniority of the company. Ensuring a culture of healthy respect for different opinion is important and the leader should give each senior member of staff enough room to voice their particular views. However, in addition to this it is crucial that once democratic agreement has been reached there is a tight agreement as to the actual delivery and evangelization of the cause. The *Boardroom Handshake* is a matter of honor and binds all to that cause above their own. All of the top team should mirror the leader's passion and indeed give out exactly the same messages. This avoids any confusion as to the correct direction of the company and all disagreement is kept away from the front line.

This obviously involves choosing the right people to work with you – not necessary yes people who do every thing you say, but professional senior members who respect management etiquette and hold the corporate cause as a priority. The leader must allow room for diversity to get the best breadth of opinion but yet channel it all into a constructive way forward.

No where is this more important than right at the top. Lord Tom Sawyer emphasizes the need for the Chair and Chief Executive to set the tone. He describes the essential mix "they speak as one, they act as one and they get that fundamental trust in what they need to do ... "

Case study comment

The boardroom handshake

"... you've got to be open and honest around the shared values, get the strategy agreed and when you do agree it, you've both got to stick to it and drive it through the business together, so that people can't see a gap between the chief exec and the chairman and they speak as one, they act as one and they get that fundamental trust in what they

▶

> need to do, then a chairman has got to have some really pretty good performance ratings for the chief executive's performance and be able to then step back a bit from that shared experience and say ok we did that together now, you're responsible for delivering on that and my job is to make sure you do it, so it's a coming together to get the vision and the mission and the strategy and then it's a stepping back a little bit ... "
>
> Lord Tom Sawyer House of Lords and ex-Chairman of The Notting Hill Housing Trust.

Polylogue (multiple dialogue)

Having secured a sound senior synchronicity, the down flow, up flow and cross flow of information is under study. More than the senior team cascading the same message, which is important, a multidirectional flow of information needs to be crafted so all aspects of the crafted future and its day-to-day mechanics can be communicated with ease and speed. In the same spirit as embracing the different views of the top team, this set-up needs to value all opinions from different levels in the organization, giving the time and comfort to surface and then channel all inputs into the best compromise possible to suit the overall cause.

A multiple dialogue or *polylogue* must be encouraged so feedback is swift and executive action then more appropriate to the business. The transparency transports information all ways and quickly so front line issues reach the top sooner and senior level messages are cascaded with a consultative approach for more effect.

The openness in its turn encourages a common line of communication which in itself encourages a commonality of direction, cause, and purpose. This does not happen by accident and needs to engineered and invited. Val Gooding expresses the need for proactivity and doggedness clearly in her bid to court opinion from the troops.

Case study comment

Invitation and RSVP

"So I think what you have to do is actively go out and ask people. So here we do a lot of measurement of, what do our employees think of us, and what do our customers think of us, and we try and make those things, not just research things but very active things. So, for example, we do an employee opinion survey every year, and even for me when I get my bit of the employee opinion survey that is about me from my top team, I will sit down with members of the team and say, 'look, it says this here and I think I should do better on this, what can we do?' I mean basically if they want to tell me something, they are not going to tell me really unless I directly ask them and look like I really want to know. So I think leaders have to ask for uncomfortable truths. Every now and again you have to remind people that you want to hear bad news, you want to hear about things where things should be done better. You have to keep saying that and reinforcing it … ."

Val Gooding, CEO, of BUPA

So open and effective communication in turn brings into play the question of structural design. It is one thing to evangelize the need to have the multidirectional dialogue but this is pointless if the corporate structure impedes its progress. From a selfish point of view Mission Command needs front line data quickly and efficiently. From a less selfish point of view speedy communication cascades are motivational. Structural design should allow the free progress of ideas, opinions, and information. Rigid hierarchical approaches may slow the flow and worse allow insecure managers within to wing clip talent and filter ideas through their and in their own preferred manner. In short the overall strategic plan and design should be solidly underpinned by a structural design which fully supports its mission and be unhindered by hierarchical blocks.

Walk the talk

Pour over the corporate structure design. Mark out communication bottlenecks in its cascade as well as along lateral lines. Evaluate how strongly it supports the strategic vision.

Hypermetropia (long-sightedness)

Long-sightedness! A long-term approach is necessary to channel all aspects of the tactical tasks of the business toward the crafted future.

As well as an overall culture of *polylogue* communication with fast feedback, the great leader must be hypermetropic with their focal point on that distant point ahead. This is not to say they don't put on the shorter-term lenses of different management tools to see the state of the business at different levels and stages, but that they ensure that all of that heads for that same focal point. Using all of the opinions and tips from the *polylogue* environment will ensure that the vision is a shared one and this in itself is a further bond and takes the eye of the follower further down the focal point as they do their day-to-day work.

Dividing the overall vision into achievable segments of achievement and pulling it all back out again is not just the job of the leader and indeed not the leader's only job. This is also necessary at all levels of leader and manager throughout the organization to ensure a culture of *visioning* is thoroughly in place and then becomes also self perpetuating.

This needs to be borne in mind at the stage of strategic design. Just as being mindful of structural design and its underpinning of the overall cause is important, so is judging and deciding on the actual design of the strategic plan and direction. As well as being forward thinking and progressive, the strategic design must contain its own underpinning of reality.

So, many levels of the crafted future arise in different places in the company and outside of the company and they all support an overall crafted future of success. The choices of the leader are key to that success, their leadership discretion a powerful tool in its own right which influences the levels of agreement and cooperation in the fabric of the organization.

Great rate

This chapter has touched on some of the elements of "crafting the future." It is not a definitive list but the elements which seem to make the extraordinary stand apart from the ordinary involve

Appealability

Boardroom Handshake

Conductor to Conduit

Destination Determination

Hypermetropia

Name and Fame

New Improved Version

Power Levers

Partnership Power

Particular Power

Personal Passion

Personality Power

Perspective Power

Polylogue

Positional Power

Professional Power

Synchronized Seniority

Transmutation

Visioning

CHAPTER 3

Surfacing sentiments

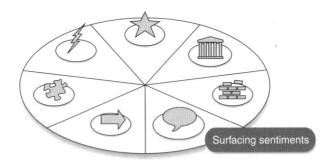

Source: Compiled by authors

Chapter introduction

Really knowing what is going on at ground level is difficult to achieve. More can be gained from being informed about the past and present so that it contributes to the future.

This is viewed through

Surfacing sentiments and their shared state
The formation of a model to show the different levels at which staff will share information depending on leader behavior

Politics and perception
Acting in appropriate ways to suit the situation and finding ways to look for information rather than wait for it

▶

Political points of difference (PPODs)

Points at which conflict occurs or may occur along a perception pathway

Personal perspectives

Appreciating the differences in the perception of each member of staff

Team tactics

Understanding that a staff member is one person individually and yet another as part of the team dynamic

Being great, visioning, and crafting the future is of little use if the leader does not step down from the ivory tower to really get a feel for the business and the people on a regular basis. This should not be a dramatic demonstration to merely look the part but a real and ongoing habit of harmony where all are naturally and organically in tune.

Equally, this should not just be an exercise in the present. It is important to surface past experiences and organically grown values and feelings within the company which have grown over time and use this information to establish the best way forward for the future. This is not just an exercise in the historical formation of the company but a real understanding of how current thinking is borne of the past and its experiences.

For any business leader it is essential to know what is going on at ground level and throughout the company. The odd token of wandering around is not going to collect the really juicy and "real" information which will make a difference to the strategic decision-making process. Employees, whether cynical or fearful of the sudden executive presence, are obviously not going to share their innermost thoughts or even their honest opinion and will inevitably say what is expected or what keeps them safe, or perhaps improve their own particular cause. Such collection of causes is bound to cascade back down the system again rather than make any real impact on the overall direction of the company. The trick for the great leader then is to have a deliberate tack to secure this valuable information in a caring way and one that is part of normal corporate practice.

Therefore, surfacing sentiments is much more than selling in the vision and inviting comment, it is about incorporating the facts and feelings of the workforce into the overall plan to contribute to that direction. Not just the facts and feelings you can see of course but also those you cannot.

Dannie Jost – Executive Leadership Consultant – comments on the presence of emotional perspective in the workplace.

Case study comment

Acknowledging different feelings

"As a consultant who often had the privilege of interviewing both sides of an issue, it was easy to have the necessary distance to see the demons plaguing the business. There is a utopia even in today's business environment that pretends that people have no sentiments and no emotions when they enter the board room, the office floor, or the assembly plant floor. Actually this corresponds to a dystopia that has been maliciously or not, labelled as a utopia. I have often wondered how so much hypocrisy has been able to infiltrate itself in the head of so many well educated, reasonably rational and apparently emotionally equilibrated people."

Dannie Jost – Executive Leadership Consultant

Token empowerment is laughable now and employees are no longer so prone to the cap tipping of the captive. They have choice, they have freedom, and they have power of their own. What they have to say is valuable and the choice of whether to say it is theirs. No cosmetics will draw it from their shrewd shoulders, they will deliver in their own time and in their own way and only once they trust the figureheads and once they feel comfortable in an environment which allows it.

To surface sentiments as effectively as possible, the great leader must think carefully about fitting themselves into the fabric of the business and its people. They must bring the past forward and place it into the current setting. Getting into the heart and mind of the business means getting into the hearts and minds of the staff. No token rolling up of sleeves or removal of jacket will be enough. The great leader should be really interested, well researched, and really care. That will show, gain trust, and then gain the real facts and feelings.

This will only occur with such an honest approach and spirit and in the right atmosphere of trust. Then the leader really sees what is actually going on right under their nose rather than risk being fed with what followers think they want to hear or need to say to protect themselves.

To start the process of drilling for this information, a keen understanding of past and present team dynamics and politics is necessary. This will help bring more productivity through the subsequent overt trust and enlightenment and hopefully this in turn will drive far less underground where covert, hidden agendas can surface as sabotage and stop those wheels turning. Equally, an honest approach by the leader is important.

Case study comment

An honest approach

"The observation is that emotional key issues are very difficult to raise. People get easily muddled within their attachment to specific concepts of proper behaviour and egocentric agendas, and very quickly forget the purpose or joint goal of the organization. Things get personal although everybody is pretending that it is just rational. In my view, this is business schizophrenia. Recognizing it and respectfully addressing it is the key. This is what I call speaking the

▶

unspeakable. Granted, it is not easy to do! To tell somebody in a meeting that perhaps their arguments are good, but that I just do not like the way they look, or how they behave, or what exactly irritates me about them or their arguments, and as a consequence I am thus not going to give them any of my support, is just not considered appropriate behaviour. Yet, this is often what is going on in people's minds and inform-ing their behaviours and decisions. There is nothing rational about this, yet people will justify whatever behaviour they do put on the table with intellectually plausible rational argumentation which in fact has nothing to do with the underlying sentiments. Yet, only the few – call them the fools, the brave, the leaders – will ever dare to voice a view that goes beyond the semblance of rationale, and go straight into the unspeakable and make the call, and address the real issue, not the apparent issues."

Dannie Jost – Executive Leadership Consultant

Walk the talk

Choose a team and investigate its history over the past several years. Assess how previous values and thinking has manifested itself today in both positive and negative ways.

Now think of a time when you should have been more honest and tackled an issue more directly.

Naturally, hidden agendas exist in all companies and at every level and it would be naïve to think that they can be eliminated completely. Part of the team drive then should contain a sharing level so all team members can say what they think openly and feel able to trust the leader's fair treatment of and use of the views given. The shared views in turn give way to the element of shared leadership where shared responsibility for actions makes way for true empowerment.

So two drilling levels are evident, that at team level, and that at individual level. Two willing levels are evident, that which can be seen and that which cannot.

These elements must be considered when surfacing sentiments and creating an environment which sustains that surfacing rather than smothering essential business indicators. Of course these indicators can surface in scientific ways such as increased staff turnover figures as dissatisfied employees vote with their feet, but even where their departure is welcome, there is no telling how much the destructive underground surprises they have left behind will eat away at the supporting structure of the company. Besides, once the scientific indictors are visible much of the harm is already done.

Surfacing sentiments starts simply by setting in a permanent accessibility both ways and an ongoing awareness of the "levels" of operation is a good guide to and a good start for a great leader so that their good intentions are not wasted. Going in with eyes, ears, and heart wide open will ensure more is surfaced willingly and so more is known to act upon.

Figure 3.1 shows clearly what can be gained from the extra effort. Facts and feelings shared willingly in a trusting environment

Surface level	Facts	Feelings	
First floor Support	Shared willingly For corporate good	Shared willingly In the spirit of trust	
Ground level Self save	Shared selectively For individual good	Shared selectively With limited trust	Line of visibility
Basement Sabotage	Shared sereptitiously For corporate harm	Shared sereptitiously With no trust	

Figure 3.1   Surfacing sentiments and their shared state

Source: Compiled by authors

and the corporate good are available to those who do the ground-work. This is the level at which the staff truly *support* the company and are in line with the overall vision and direction as what they say contributes directly to it as does how happy they are. If they become less happy about events, then again the accessible environment allows them to share this openly and issues are nipped in the bud before they have a chance to become invisible and inwardly destructive for both the member of staff and the organization. Val Gooding, CEO of BUPA, makes it clear that leaders should be ready to take uncomfortable news or facts about themselves graciously.

Case study comment

Be ready to hear bad news well

"I mean basically if they want to tell me something, they are not going to tell me really unless I directly ask them and look like I really want to know. So I think leaders have to ask for uncomfortable truths. Every now and again you have to remind people that you want to hear bad news, you want to hear about things where things should be done better. You have to keep saying that and reinforcing it."

Val Gooding, CEO, BUPA

Some sentiments can be surfaced at the *self-save* level but these are very selective as staff only share what they need to. At this level, they may work competently as focus on task completion is the driver for them but synergy is not achieved as an autono-mous state gives little or no extra to the company they work for. Staff left to operate at this level, whether deliberately or perhaps through ignorance by the leader, will only do what they have to, say what they have, and share what they have to. Some may regard this as satisfactory, but what a waste. The particular expertise of that frontline person is kept contained and not released for the benefit of the company. The full ability of that member of staff is not utilized so they too miss out on opportunities to develop their thinking and practices for their own furtherment. In all, no real loyalty exists to the leader or the corporate direction.

Below ground lies the devil in the detail. A subterranean layer of sabotage swirls beneath the surface. At the *sabotage* level, energies have turned inwards and downwards. No trust exists between employee and leader, so facts and feelings are shared elsewhere. Dissatisfied employees are not necessarily nasty. The innocent sharing of disappointment and dissatisfactions can be just as harmful as any deliberate spite.

Where no open chance to talk is given, staff will naturally gather to support each other. This support becomes their own first floor level of those listed in Figure 3.1 and notably the company is absent from its members. The staff then form their own layers of self-save and sabotage and this then in turn creates itself again in further and further subdivision of loyalties. Survival of the individual is higher on the agenda than corporate competitive advantage.

The not so great leader and the company are now CCJ'd! The Coffee Cup Jury is powerful and can heavily influence the workings of the company. Gatherings in the kitchen give staff the opportunity to talk freely with each other or in groups they prefer. Sentiments will surface here before anywhere else. The CCJ is not to be underestimated and the wise and politically sound leader will keep it well fed with positive things to pass between them. In America, it is the Water Cooler where the gathering occurs. Same concept though – being aware of, and in some control of, the informal communications and petty politics of the organization is key to surfacing the sentiments and ensuring that they are surfaced at the right level. The great leader must consider this for the present while evaluating how the accumulation of such behavior and beliefs over time affect the thinking now.

Walk the talk

Randomly select five of your staff and be honest with yourself. Measure their relationship with you using Figure 3.1.

▶

At which level do they operate? What can you do to improve the situation and encourage them to surface their sentiments?

Go and ask three people you do not know very well in the company what you can do to improve things.

Politics and perception

In addition to having an awareness and ongoing instinct as to levels of information release to surface sentiments, the great leader should give consideration to how those views and differences form in the first place. Previous values and ways of doing things will have an effect on current practice and thinking as well as current individual perceptions. The leader then must work through in their own mind how these views and differences, past and present, may manifest themselves in the physical and emotional workplace they must deal with now. Having a good Political Quotient (PQ) to perceive it in the first place is essential and then of course to weave it all into the corporate fabric.

Making the effort to perceive and understand the different sentiments in the system will reveal the rich diversity of position and opinion not just in relation to the overall corporate cause but also to each other.

A further bridging role emerges. Already a custodian of the main bridge between the vision and the workforce, the great leader must now plan the necessary tributary bridges leading into it. Promotion of the overall cause is only one part of the role as history, subcauses, differences, and autonomous agendas need to be appreciated.

Being different should be allowed. Voicing an opinion should be easy and without critical judgment. In essence, getting the buy in from staff involves actually buying into their differences and allowing the room for them. Coercion and cutting off have no place in equitable and empathic leadership.

Clever and considered, rather than coercive, use of power balanced with political prowess becomes a combination more likely to bring out the best in the workforce. This helps line them up with the vision as well as spot any potential issues so that they can be smoothed out early or prevented altogether.

It can be tempting to overlook arguments within the workforce, as they may seem too troublesome or too petty and perhaps even deliberately avoid the negativity. Such a burying of one's head in the sand though does not mean issues disappear – they simply find another venue and get bigger left to their own devices.

Walk the talk

Have you ever avoided being involved with conflicts at work between staff? If so, think back through it all carefully. How could your diplomatic intervention have helped the situation be resolved?

It is best then to tackle politics head on with a positive attitude and turn the issues into upward facing and open opportunities to avoid further delay or destruction of progress. Each political issue is just the tip of a large iceberg so is in effect a gift to the leader as a warning of deeper issues. If each one is seen as a positive opportunity to become involved with the business at ground level with a solution-focused approach, then there is a greater likelihood of achieving a level of cooperation which suits all parties with the least amount of tension and the best compromise as a coalition rather than certain individuals making more compromise than others and breeding a smoldering resentment which will surface eventually anyway.

This political adeptness is not necessarily a natural skill and will need to be cultivated and worked on constantly by any leader professing to be great. It is one thing to spot it and that can be hard enough, but it is quite another to find the right level for peace when agendas are so diverse and at different visibility levels themselves. A true valuing of the diversity must occur and an empathic ability to think each matter through with the mind of the employee as well as the mind of the custodian of the organization. Personal discipline comes into play as does a level of robustness.

The reward is high though and once mindsets are influenced in a positive and productive way, all benefit and all face the same direction toward the overall vision.

Complacency caution must be exercised, however, as the political needs of individuals, teams, and the organization itself need to line up with each other. This is more than complicated enough but if you then add to it the ever-changing and organic needs of each individual in their respective work environments, in their teams, and then contextualize that with previous values within the organization as well as the present, things become very convoluted. Political sensitivity is necessary at many levels and must be ongoing. It is required at many levels and must be partnered with power levers to create the right combination of security and trust for the employee to operate comfortably within.

Walk the talk

Working with a list of your staff or a company organogram, grade yourself out of ten for each member in terms of how well you understand their personal needs at work.

Once it is understood that real movement forward involves this complicated balance and keeping different individuals happy in their roles in corporate direction, progress is made. Each gentle and subtle push is complemented by another in a different way but in the same direction and ground is covered. This takes time and patience not only in probing to perceive but also in practicing to please, but if movement is solidly and permanently forward speed is less important. Besides, once this motion is started it will also become self-perpetuating in some parts and therefore gains momentum – in the right direction and in one direction. Once the great leader sees the result of their investment in terms of patience, time, and understanding, they will repeat the process and become more capable and more perceptive. This makes the impact they have on the business a formidable prospect in the best way.

If each gentle and subtle push is counteracted by an aggravated pull in the opposite direction, then of course no ground is made. Worse still, if the pull is stronger in its negativity than the push is with its positivity, then a vicious trip downwards is inevitable. This weakens corporate strength and competitive advantage from within, draining it of vital energy which should be used to keep out the competition.

Political points of difference (PPODs)

In terms of thinking ahead and planning productivity, it is a question of identifying the *Political Points of Difference* (PPODs; Figure 3.2) within the informal structures of the organization. These are the particular joining points of paradox where most tension will occur and will be similar in most organizations so can be planned for. Five clear perception pathways exist in the communication lines of a typical organization.

On these five paths differences will occur in terms of views and opinions. These clashes will then create opportunity for

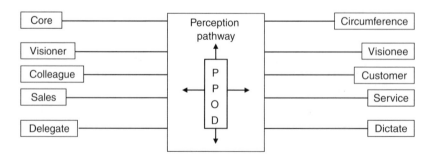

Figure 3.2   Perception pathways and PPODs

Source: Authors

argument and rather than allow the sentiments to burrow under-ground and influence the political security, these PPODs can be used as viewing stations where problems can be revealed and then dealt with. Better still, the issues can be embraced and made part of a positive way forward. So, the deliberate act of looking as if by magic increases the perception of the great leader and more is dealt with at source and used in a way which is constructive to the overall needs of the company.

Let's look at each of the five a little more closely to increase the value from each viewing point.

Core, circumference

It is inevitable that a point of political difference is going to occur between the central strategic core of the business and the path to the circumference where messages have been passed on and translated many fold. The particular point will depend on the size of the company and its communications systems and structure. As well as translation issues there may also simply be differences in opinion along this pathway. Diplomatic step-ins can prevent irritation either way and a "them and us" culture evolving to the point of no return. It is common for head office staff to be much maligned by those in the field and for those operations staff to be suspicious of those at the core.

Naturally, each party is starting by facing the opposite direction to the other. Core staff at the center of the strategic cause face inwards and have the shareholders in mind along with other external stakeholders. Operations staff face outwards along the path to the circumference attending to marketing, financial, and sales issues. A key learning point here for the leader is that the stretched and opposing energies pull apart from each other and weaken the company cohesion.

Effort by the great leader to ensure each party looks in the other directions too and understands the different agendas, even if they do not agree with them, so that they can be incorporated into a profitable corporate compromise, is well worth the thought and application time, and energy.

Visioner, visionee

In terms of pure role difference, the leader or visioner tends to have a positional power over the visionee so the resulting relationship can develop another PPOD for a number of reasons. These are not necessarily the obvious ones of power abuse but perhaps of confusions in how much authority the manager level is given to complete their tasks. If managers are not given enough authority to get things done, subordinates will rebel or niche and if they then find themselves sandwiched between an invisible insubordination from below and accountability pressures from above, a large PPOD will develop here.

Add this to the complicated nature of personal relationships between boss and subordinate and many areas of conflict become evident.

The great leader not only looks for this potential PPOD but also looks at ways to prevent it occurring at all from the beginning. Even as a new leader with no personal history within the company, it is important to research and appreciate the history of events which face the individual. Those leaders with a personal history at the company could find tensions could occur for instance where they have been promoted over others in the team they came from so a political prowess is very important in making the "rejected" candidate still feel an important member of the team and a valued ally rather than sport the new power over them in what they may view as a humiliating come down. These sensitivities are often missed in business and cause no end of disruption. With a little intellectual investment though relationships can be cultivated where respect is earned rather than demanded and communication then flows that bit more overtly and freely. Key learning objectives in this pathway for perception then are about trust, earned respect, and empathy.

Colleague, customer

Beyond the Circumference lies the customer. In the same way as mentioned before where the Core-based staff face one way and operations face the other, the same can occur if the leader thinks through a perception pathway line from the colleague level within those operations and extends it right outside to the customer. This is different to Core to Circumference in that it starts later down the line and flies in a different level or at a different height in terms of strategic overview. Nevertheless, it is just as important.

This level/height takes into account internal comfort zones on one side and customer satisfaction on the other. Belonging, status, systems, procedures etc are all important internally. Staff can be influenced by the beliefs of others at their level and work toward peer inclusion rather than exclusion in some circumstances. This may be more important in their eyes and to their survival than overall corporate cause.

Those whose starting point is the customer may show some disdain for the internal processes such as meetings, procedures, audits, and so on, which seem tiresome to them. Both are essential to the business but both create a PPOD at some point in the pathway. Internal networking and external networking become two different things, again facing in different directions, when really all are customers to the great leaders and treated as such. A strike for external independence clashes with a need for internal collegiate interdependence and these petty politics affect the profit margin.

The great leader will help all look both ways again focusing as much on internal issues as external. With no poor cousin emerging from the diplomatic process both sets can provide more lateral thinking and the great leader can link these together. Key learning objectives in this pathway for perception then are more about understanding the need for some subordinates to fit into their environment against the need for those who start with customer satisfaction as their foothold.

Hans Blix pinpointed more than a few PPODs when he was tasked to inspect Iraqi territory for weapons. From an internal perspective he faced intensive political intervention from many angles in matters such as choosing trusted team members and from an external perspective customers such as the press provided an extra degree of pressure on their performance.

Case study comment

Pressed in all directions!

"Both Colin Powell and Condoleezza Rice were interested in placing an American in my office and said as much to me. They expressed their wishes but they both realized that they could not do anything without our decision. They knew what my position was: I was responsible to the Security Council, not just to them. I certainly said so – politely. We followed our line. What we found, when it got hotter, was that the American media would attack us. We were sort of skinned alive by the media when we did not follow the US line. Sometimes they said 'you seemed to support us and help us, but now we don't know where you are'. They expected us to be on their side. We were not. We were servants of the Security Council. Occasionally we could see that the US administration dropped hints to the media leading them to attack us fiercely. They did so, for instance, in February or early March 2003. The Americans had got a picture of an old cluster bomb and they also had suspicions that Iraq had drones that could be used for the dispersion of biological weapons. We doubted both. I have discussed both cases in my book 'Disarming Iraq'. The US Administration asked 'why have you failed to report this' and a gang of media rushed in and claimed that we were suppressing information. So, through the Administration's links to media pressure was exercised."

Hans Blix, responsible for UN weapons inspections in Iraq

Sales, service

Perhaps the best way to look at this particular perception pathway to pinpoint the potential PPOD is to think of sales as a short-term driver and service as a long-term investment.

Anyone who has been in sales knows when there is a special buzz and that a winning mentality and competitive spirit are key to success. League tables and targets provide direction. These will have been devised originally to fit in with the overall corporate vision and targets, so in a way are contributing to the overall cause. However, the individual, team, or unit drive toward their gain is less corporate in spirit. The target is the end goal in their eyes and all drive stops there. This is not to take away the crucial contribution these sales make and without these short-term blasts the overall figures would be less. It is important to recognize the need for the great leader to surface sentiments at the PPOD though in that this more excited and quick fix focus may conflict with that of the service driven individual with a longer-term mind.

Those with a service focus are more likely to form relationships with customers with a quality driver. They are unlikely to sell the customer anything that they do not need and will try to tailor the company to serve the customer not the other way around. This is not anti-corporate and very valuable in its own right as loyal customers are likely to buy more from the company in the long run anyway. There is no question that this is of great worth to the business, its issue really only arises from its potential clash with the fast fix needed by the sales targets.

Both are valid and both are valuable to the company but in their different process they are bound to conflict at some point. It is the job of the great leader to anticipate this implosion and prevent the valuable energies being wasted on internal argument.

Key learning points in this perception pathway lie with lining up sectional targets to the overall cause and matching the pursuit of short-term profit with long-term customer loyalty.

Delegate, dictate

Levels of authority vary in different structures and with different leaders. There will be times when direction is appropriate and times when delegation is appropriate. Again, how these are used rather than abused is essential to the smooth running of the organization and the amount of conflict within. Getting the pitch right then is key to that success so the great leader needs to pinpoint this particular PPOD along this perception pathway with extra care as this is perhaps even more difficult to guess than some of the other PPODs mentioned.

Delegation and true empowerment are strong forces which can benefit individuals and subsequently the organization they work for. Delegating and empowering a member of staff appropriately can develop them and create a spirit of positive productivity. The point at which the receipt of such duties is a pleasure and a benefit or an impertinent push on a member of staff's goodwill is a PPOD to isolate to surface particular sentiments which may make a difference to organizational performance. Pitching it wrong can create resentment.

Equally, not delegating and empowering enough can do the same. If jobs are always delegated to the same individual or there is a "cherry picking" system, potentially useful staff may feel underused and developed and resent the favoritism elsewhere.

How important an individual feels is important in itself. The importance of the task level they have been instructed to undertake, the peer and superior recognition they gain from undertaking it, the sense of personal development without an overriding fear of failure are all key in ensuring that the right sentiments are set.

Key learning points in this perception pathway lie then with the choice of levels of empowerment and delegating to develop individuals (see Table 3.1).

Table 3.1   Key learning observations on the perception pathways

Perception		Pathway	Key learning observations
Core	to	Circumference	Different agendas
			Different directions
Visioner	to	Visionee	Levels of trust and respect
			Understanding
			Empathy
Colleague	to	Customer	Peer inclusion
			Customer satisfaction
Sales	to	Service	Line up targets to overall cause
			Short-term profit
			Long-term customer loyalty
Delegate	to	Dictate	Empowerment levels
			Employee development

Walk the talk

Follow each of the five perception pathways and isolate at least two PPODs along each. Table 3.1 lists the positive actions you will then implement to prevent any conflict or to reduce any that exists already.

It is clear then that as well as PPODs in certain pathways at organizational level being revealed, an understanding of the individual and their personal team standing must also be present in the leader to truly surface sentiments from their valued staff. This is a different level of looking and needs to be examined separately.

Personal perspectives

Individual difference is perhaps a PPOD of its own and a potentially explosive one if overlooked. All visions and strategies cascaded by the directorate will be translated many times by individual perception. This is not just whether they agree with it or not, but how they fear it will affect them in their particular roles in the company. Drilling down to this level of individual understanding is key to surfacing sentiments to a level where they can be safely dealt with – or even better embraced and valued.

The shared purpose of the corporate vision can be a great thing to be part of for the individual but that is only one part of their need. They need to feel a real part of it and that their view counts in the overall cause.

Managing diversity has taken on new meanings in latter years. Where it started highlighting the benefits of embracing ethnic, cultural, gender, age differences, it has now progressed. More than the simple differences of religion, race, and so on there is now a need to embrace the difference in each person in terms of their personality, learning, and development. What is even more important now is that each person is appreciated for their individual difference not just their ethnicity, age, or gender. Previous appreciation by category was good in its time and did a lot of good but pigeon holing people is not going to really appreciate their true individual difference and gain their willing spirit for added synergy in the organization.

This is not to say that everything is wrong with corporate uniformity borne of structural centralization. Belonging and setting standards are important but the message is that it should not be at the price of individuality which can be of great benefit to the great leader. Robotrons will only provide what they are programmed with. Freer spirits should be allowed to fly around to an extent to release that individual energy into the company they work for. They will only use it elsewhere if you do not anyway – positively as a hobby outside or negatively as elaborate and creative sabotage.

Back to pigeon holing or stereotyping, this can also be dangerous in terms of restricting what some individuals may be able to acquire in the way of skills. If they are categorized as one thing – they may not experiment in another area of the company. Keeping an open mind will surface more than their sentiments – it may also surface hidden talents.

The happier an individual is being themselves within the security of the corporate umbrella, the more each is likely to get from the bargain and the longer they are likely to stick with each other. This in its turn brings benefits of further experience and wisdom being contained in the company and not trotting off to benefit the competition.

Team tactics

Protecting the PPOD of individual difference then provides a window into a different level of observation the great leader must undertake. The respect for individual direction lies at one level of observation and can be linked with the company direction for best effect. At another level though, the same individual has to interact with other individuals of different levels in the company and as part of their team. The individual and the organization may have a very different dynamic to the individual and the team – and then of course there is the team and the organization dynamic too.

However successful the individual relationship is with the organization, there is no guarantee that team dynamics will also not play a part in creating further political issues. Another PPOD exists between the individual and the team and then one between the team and the company.

Acceptance in one's peer group is a big deal for most. Some can be very different on their own compared to how they work in a team. Working with difference now extends to the ability or inability of the other team members to accept the differences. Belonging at another level is important to the individual team member not wanting to be left out.

The great leader not only needs to surface the sentiments of the individual then but also to surface the sentiments of the team within which they work. Seeing the individual personality defaults or single behavior clusters in group context is an important part of making sure one is educated enough a leader to make the best decisions possible and to be of the best service possible.

Isolating any PPODs here will help form better working bonds which stand a better chance of standing the test of time, change, and pressure.

The team itself is a mini-organization within the large one. If it becomes inward fighting and inward looking then it is more than likely to pull the overall corporate cause in the wrong direction. At the very least, the lack of appropriate direction for the energies of the team will weaken the overall fabric of the hosting organization.

Better then that all face the same way and once the PPOD is observed at team level, an acceptance of a structured settling period for the different individuals will help. Inevitably, each team member must find and be happy with their team space and duties and feel satisfied and proud at peer level. This will then feed into a higher level of satisfaction linked to the overall corporate cause. The great leader can help furnish this process. By allowing some healthy and constructive surfacing of sentiments – peer to peer – the team will more quickly settle and an avoidance of the perpetual arguing of individuals will be avoided. This will also prevent negative sentiments going underground.

Once this is observed and time invested in trying to get it right, the job does not stop there. There are many teams to consider, functions/departments, and so on which must all work with each other and the same rules apply at yet another level.

Conclusion

It is more than evident that surfacing sentiments involves a multi level and 360 degree approach. In addition, once spotted, saved, invested in, there is no rest. New situations occur every day to change the dynamic so the process of **PPOD** spotting or casting needs to be an ongoing one. The great leader needs to create a system of checks to look for the potential political conflicts and the opportunities to surface sentiments. Such a system of "looking lines" or perception pathways draws a map of potential issues so that plans can be made and allies can be brought on board to help scout for issues in the same way. Even the greatest leader cannot be in all places in any one time so needs help to sustain the process. This reduces the quantity of nasty surprise and also improves status so the leader and the organization are better placed to cope with them.

It is also evident that the great leader must have high levels of respect for the differences of their staff. Valuing their diversity in all senses and incorporating it into the overall corporate body stand more chance of success.

Great rate

This chapter has touched on some of the elements of "surfacing sentiments". It is not a definitive list but the elements which seem to make the difference involve:

360 degree Approach

Different Agendas

Empathy

Employee Development

Empowerment Levels

Perception Pathway

Political Points of Difference

Political Quotient

Shared Views

CHAPTER 4

Finding ways through

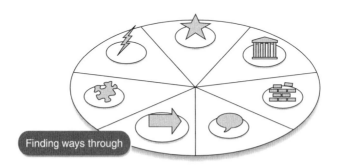

Source: Compiled by authors

Chapter introduction

Visible vision vectors
Bringing the vision to life through and at al levels of the organization

The processes of strategic choice
Leadership discretion under pressure. Making the right structural choices to align the business with the vision

The strategic choice processes
Assessing the range of systems, processes, and people and aligning their day-to-day roles to the chosen structures and therefore to the overall vision

Ethical edification
Influencing the ethical soft structure with the correct organizational moral values

The cultural carriageway
A pathway to isolating the keystones of a cultural soft structure

Having looked at the inner core of the leader, established the need to "vision", and drilled into the soft fabric of the enterprise to surface sentiments, the need for strong underpinning becomes evident if truly great leadership has foundation. This underpinning in terms of the strength of the corporate structure and its ability to hold up the vision can make the difference between falling short of, or achieving, the strategic direction. So not only does the great leader need the "spirit" to succeed but also the "spine" in more ways than one. This spine is not just the obstinate doggedness and strength of the leader themselves but the strength of the corporate structures holding it up to the competition.

This thinking takes us to more visible territory. We travel from feelings to actual frameworks. From the decisions of strategic choice and direction to the design of corporate structure to achieve it, to the day-to-day processes and systems which provide the core products or services, the leader's influence on these multilevel management issues will make the difference between success and failure.

Top-down or bottom-up approaches matter little here as long as the whole of the structural design, or perhaps redesign, ensures an agility and flexibility in the marketplace and helps the leader find ways through key challenges. Each part of that structure must be strong to hold up the other parts.

Less instantly visible areas such as cultural issues may need to be tackled and ethical dilemmas may occur and this is where leadership choice differentiates the great from the not so great. It is the ability of the leader to make the right choices and keep everyone and everything facing in the same direction which tips the balance.

Management of the transactional matters of the business at its different mechanical levels means more than a little wandering around. A real insight into the detail of the operations and systems is as important as an insight into the feelings of the workforce if visions are to be achieved. Making the vision visible at all of these levels means more than reinterpreting the evangelization to different audiences, although that too is important. It means translating the whole of the vision and its parts into the mechanical at the many needed levels of operation.

Visible vision vectors

Vectorization of the vision will inevitably court paradox and politics. *Political Points of Difference* (PPODs) will occur at many three-dimensional points as business decisions have to be made which start defining the leadership gap between one vectoral interest and another. Differences will occur in many ways as discussed in the previous chapter so ensuring the structural design and processes within support and enhancing the whole strategic process becomes a clever balancing act between purpose and practicality.

The great leader needs to study the existing vectors with a 360 degree eye and isolate the PPODs. This time though, in addition to ensuring that the human relationships are intact at these points, it is necessary to ponder on the structure and processes and audit their robustness for the purpose. Systems, procedures, and the mini hierarchical structures are all part of the big picture in their own way and their overview and review is very important in terms of ensuring that they are a duct to the main cause and any potential blocks are dealt with.

Particular thought must be invested in bringing the overall vision into visible translation at the practical and structural levels. There will be gaps in the existing structures which must be filled. Mission milestones will be missing in certain areas. Starting at the beginning of every hierarchy, at the beginning of every process and at the beginning of every procedure and asking what that point does for the overall vision, what practical purpose does it serve toward the overall cause, and what *mission milestones* it provides along the way.

Walk the talk

Having assessed whether current systems and processes are up to the job – isolate five new areas where processes will need to be created to uphold the vision.

Pinpoint three new mission milestones you can introduce to the structure.

This "frame" for future fortuity will then not only provide the structural base for a stronger establishment but also catch anything collectively covert and potentially damaging to the company. The PPODs as such become audit stops where all levels can measure their progress toward the overall destination and discussions can occur regarding the improvement of the processes as well as assist in the building of good human relations and communication.

Such structural back up is a necessity for the leader, as this level of in-depth insight into the business cannot be achieved by charisma alone or even just by wandering around and being seen to take an interest. Not only does such an approach offer up many an opportunity for a detailed look at the business at many of its ground levels and beyond, it also compensates in many ways for the awkwardness that the pure human relationship level can restrict "real" communication. This is not to say that surfacing sentiments and having an open human relationship with staff is not key to success, but it in itself and used by itself will not be enough. Even with good relations between leader and subordinate, psychological barriers can occur. Even with an open invite to say what you think in the working environment – there is no guarantee that the majority will do so.

The internal openness is one thing but the leader will at some points have to make decisions perhaps in terms of costs, which will be a necessary but perhaps unpopular move. Great leadership is not just about gaining the short-term vote; it is also about ensuring that all arrive at the destination safely. Sometimes there will be a paradox between desire and the necessary, or keeping people happy in the short term and keeping to the overall target. As this is likely rather than just possible, it is important to cater around its occurrence. Sound structure will ensure differences are aired and compromises met. Structure headed in the corporate direction will help contain covert practices as well as uncover them.

The processes of strategic choice

As well as hold up the vision and make that vision visible to the staff and to the outside world, the choice of strategic direction is made essentially to beat the competition. All too often though a new "broom" sweeps into the organization and one of the biggest impacts they can make is to restructure the organization. In some cases, this is the correct action to take but in others the action is premature and more demonstrative than effective.

Visualizing the vision in terms of hard choice and structure takes some homework. In this instance, things are more scientific and some deliberate homework needs to be done. There are no rocket science suggestions here. The homework is simple and essentially data led.

Starting with the good old environmental analysis gives the essential basics. Most know this and even sigh an "of course" at its suggestion. What would be interesting though is the frequency of use and the accuracy and actual use of such simple but effective tools for fuelling the choice processes.

The competitor analysis accompanies this and should be done hand in hand and frequently. Again, this tool is usually in the executive portfolio and aired regularly, but it is an idea to really study how effectively it is being applied and how up to the minute the information is. The key is to accept that the data collected from these stalwarts ages incredibly quickly so the advice is not so much about using the tools we know are already there but checking how often and how effectively they are actually being used.

Therefore, we have an up to date and solid platform of *history and mystery shopping* and this data will feed the strategic choice toward the vision. And what choice! The great leader stands in front of many options but the price for choosing the wrong option is high. The dilemma dissecting the decision-making process is ever present so the responsibility levels are as high as they possibly could be. Choosing whether to jump onto the conveyor belt of price wars, to focus on customer service, to furnish flexibility of product or service, to attack a new market niche, to invest in innovation, to specialize in one area, to drill into the details of purchase access, guarantees, delivery, marketing and it goes on.

Then, as if that was not complicated enough, there could be a strategic combination/mix of these choices. The balance of this mix could be a Da Vinci Code challenge. Again, there is the increase in success if all is aligned to objectives. Picking the closest match to the overall direction and objectives sounds obvious, but often other things influence the Executive mind. Compromises sometimes have to be made between what is exactly the match for the long-term vision and what suits the short-term performance criteria.

Walk the talk

Using your recent SWOT and environmental analysis data – (if it is over three months old – refresh it) – take a strategic choice different to that which you are currently practicing and work through its merits. Does it match with your current practice, exceed it, or confirm that you have chosen the right route? If you operate a mix – naturally choose a different mix to complete the comparison process.

The structural design often aligns objectives with practices. Whether, re-layering, de-layering, right sizing, down sizing, flattening, fattening, redivisioning, redefining, redeploying, or any other kind of "ing," the decision should be data led rather than change for the sake of it or to demonstrate the presence of a new CEO.

The objectives mentioned can also be of a wide range in themselves, adding to the complication of cracking the code. The objectives to suit fulfilling the vision may be profit led or market share led, or perhaps a reputation for the best and within each of these paths will be many choices too.

From data and environment analyses to acknowledging and evaluating the strategic and objective choices to fit the vision we arrive finally at the educated place where structural design is the next consideration.

From an obvious SWOT of the current situation, the great leader will not simply look at what needs changing but at what is already good and look at ways of avoiding radical change where possible. What is actually needed rather than what is fashionable or what will look good is the key consideration for long-term success rather than short-term shelf life survival. The cynicism aroused by yet another structural change by yet another new broom must cost companies millions just in terms of the reluctance of the staff from their resulting lack of confidence.

The structural design will then evolve from these many decisions but further, the leader must still stop and take into account the existing informal structures as well as the ethical and cultural soft structures. These can be highly productive and are therefore best preserved within any new hierarchical framework. Of course changes in divisions, areaisations, vertical reporting layers, and so on may be deliberate in their attempt to eradicate the more negative informal structures which may impede progress and positive movement toward change.

In all, the great leader has the duty of *strategic alignment*. Their evaluation of the soft and hard structures and the internal and external environments is key to their effectiveness in terms of strategic planning and choice. It is the balance of all which is important rather than the most demonstrative route by the new leader. It can be seen that there are many areas within the layers of all these choices themselves and how they line up to the vision or not. In fact, one small wrong move and the whole is very much affected. Needless to say, the harder the leader works at getting it right in the most informed way possible – the "luckier" they seem to get making the right decisions.

Case study comment

Cascading the clarity

"I think it's helped now that we've literally gone back to basics and documented everything. We've agreed what Committees there will be; we've agreed their terms of reference; how much delegated power different bodies will have; all of that which was done on a bit of a wing and a prayer before. So we've got that far. But now we're back to the really big issue which is basic relationships. Now we actually do need to spend a lot more time building that understanding in a practical day to day basis and making it work in practice. A lot of that just needs a little bit of time out and little bit more of the sort of away days that we've already been doing. Taking time out to explore things is important but some of the Executive feel it is a diversion from the root cause of Shelter. But we've got to do it and I still think now we're putting in a new Chair it remains a difficult challenge."

And would you make that almost one of the prime responsibilities of the new Chair, the building of relationships?

"Yes, absolutely, yes."

Baroness Maggie Jones, Trustee of Shelter

The strategic choice processes

From the visualization of the vision at a more strategic level where strategic alignment has been discussed from the top down, we go onto organizing the organization at a more operational level. The actual reporting lines or *Hierarchical design*, the *Internal and external relationships* which result and the *Processes, communication, and controls* within those enact the strategic alignment at local level and make the difference between success and failure. Competitive advantage is gained if the structure, and so on is robust enough to support the degree of flexibility necessary to change quickly and ahead of others.

Hierarchical design

The structural framework shapes the vision and all strategic processes from its operational level in terms of the strength, support, and speed it furnishes. It is these factors that the great leaders consider when assessing its current value and aligning it to organizational challenges and objectives. Whether functions such as finance should be segregated for simplicity, clearer definition, more intense expertise, and accountability at the expense of inter-functional integration and corporate wholeness is a typical dilemma facing the leader. Equally, the organization whose structure is divided through area, product, or service for flexibility and specialization may be doing so with the cost of duplication and bad communication. Where hybrids of functional and area/product division occur in matrix form, project focus or team skill base, a range of management issues arise. The benefits of spreading the knowledge/expertise through the company to increase its flexibility and competitive advantage by significant amounts can be counteracted by the obvious result that such structural forms will "slow" down communication and decision-making processes, not to mention the potential increase in conflict opportunities and decrease in clarity of control. Stretch this all up to think globally and international competence across many cultures has its counter measure in terms of how responsive the company then remains at local/national level.

Each structural form has its own strengths and weaknesses. Functional structures certainly pool those functional disciplines such as finance, HR, sales, operations, research into focused and efficient departments. This ensures that this sectional knowledge and expertise is stored in one place and staff know where to find it as well as have the reassurance that the same standards apply to all. Departmentalizing tasks and functions consolidates set activities for greater efficiency for the organization and staff in the organization are clear that the functional section has the skill set they need for certain things and that the service has one set standard from the company overall as that function. This efficiency can be counterbalanced, however, by departmental loyalties, cultures, and efforts staying inwardly focused and communication between these different departments in the organizations can be stifled and cause misunderstanding and subsequent inefficiency. They can become too independent of the business as a whole and such functional fencing can make departments become more procedural rather than service focused toward the overall vision and aims of the organization.

Product structures ensure a similar expertise focus but based around product knowledge and expertise. Such structures have the strengths of giving in-depth knowledge again but this time more outward facing for the customer. It is reassuring for that customer to have this on tap, and further the product itself benefits from expert refinement as well as appropriate technical support. This creates a confidence at point of purchase and such strong knowledge-driven back up can ensure recommendations for further business. However, as with functional segregation, a similar stifling can occur with this set up as only having knowledge in one product area may limit the internal flexibility of a member of staff to cover in other areas. Staff can become so expert in one particular area as to be nonexpert in others, thus depriving the business of a certain fluidity. This could even further impede the staff member's own development within the whole organization as it limits their search for future promotion by keeping it contained within one particular area.

Geography, areaisation, or divisions attached to regional individuals have the advantage of a different kind of focus to bring about results. Manageable pieces of the business are run separately to corporate targets. This does have the benefit of ensuring the dedicated leadership layers keep in touch with the frontline side of the structure and this helps better tailoring of products or service for the "local" customer which may be different nationally or worldwide. The speed of reaction to local customer change is naturally much more reactive with set ups like this and decisions are more directly informed from the sources of consumer. It is common for such forms to have their own functional support services within the "local" unit and this gives a further strength of speed and customization for anything which occurs. This focus does have the benefit of directly meeting direct consumer requirements and the customer or service user has the comfort of knowing that there is an approachable person to talk to if they need to. However, internal competition can result as areas are run to their own rules but are compared with each other on league table type operations. There is a point at which this is healthy and fun and there is a point where this can backfire. Region competes against region, branch against branch, and each "locality" becomes an autonomous unit in their own right with all the disadvantages that contains as with product and functional division. There is also an increased instance of duplicity as each locality has its own administrative support and functions. Although they may do an extremely good job for the local operation, there is no guarantee that this reflects a national or international corporate norm or even that it definitely lines up with the overall vision and strategic plan. Communication between areas can become weak and this essentially creates several companies within one big company.

Matrix structures divide staff into project and multiple foci providing a wealth of personal development opportunity for individual staff members not to mention good internal exposure and opportunity. Based on projects, groups are formed to perform to budgets and deadlines to complete a part of the overall vision. Wonderful opportunities for personal achievement can arise as individuals get the chance to shine and make an impact within these substructural submarines. Time is dedicated toward a particular cause giving direction, motivation, and a sense of urgency. The organization gets a fluidity of its talent and expertise and this is used where it counts for the highest and best impact. However, these project-based structures can become quite complicated and put conflicting pressure on the same fluid individuals owning the movable talent. These individuals may find that they have many "bosses" pressing for their time and conflicts of interest may occur within the operational workings of the organization. Equally, the speed of getting things done in a matrix set up can be infuriating. It does seem that a handful of people needs to be consulted over the simplest thing, and this in turn can delay reaction to change as well as tempt the project team to become inward looking rather than outward facing.

It could be held that most corporate structures today are in fact derivations of this matrix approach and many are hybrids of several of these approaches. It would be rare to find that an organization is completely one of the described categories. Organizations want the fluidity of talent so have project-based hierarchies within, but yet may still have a product based, geography based or functional based configuration. Some of this is a product of evolution and some a product of more radical structural design. Either way such hybrids of this matrix structure can vary widely. They can be a hybrid of different balances of functional division and project division and can range from a functional manager staffing many projects with the same expert staff to a project manager controlling and incorporating the functional expertise as necessary. These ever evolving and differently balanced derivations of matrix and functional hybridity are the norm in today's changing organizational environment.

Also while the actual structural design is important and the soft structure mentioned supporting them are key to their upholding, so is the drive to make them work from the top. Dedicated interest and enthusiasm must be present not just at design stage but also through and past implementation.

This could also be affected by the relationship right at the top of that hierarchy or right in the pivotal core of that matrix – that of the Chairman and the CEO. The levels of freedom afforded to the latter may vary according to the levels if interaction of the former and this partnership has its own cascading effect on the subsequent layers.

With all of this in mind, identifying the most appropriate form of structure above is difficult and of course, it will never be as straightforward as the examples above. When assessing functional, divisional, skills teams, projects, nations, global presence, and so on, as well as aligning the structural design to the overall purpose, the competitive advantage must be assessed in terms of speed of operation and flexibility in fast changing external environments. Then, when that is on blueprint, the leader must assess how the current structure stands against that and what constructive changes needs to be made, and whether those changes need to be radical or evolve on current strengths. Indeed, the existing structure will greatly influence what is desirable and what is actually possible.

Therefore, the test is whether the structure

- aligns with the corporate objectives and overall vision,
- gains competitive advantage,
- is possible from the current structure status and available human resource,
- can mobilize and remobilize expertise,
- constructs communication conduits which pull the company together and banishes blockages in the line management hierarchies,
- provides clear responsibility portfolios for the players,
- adapts to fast changing external environments.

Walk the talk

Apply the above test criteria to your structure or indeed your structural plans.

Internal and external relationships

External relationships
This leads nicely onto the relationships which form around the structural design. The shipping in of talent or outsourcing brings

its own issues to add to the leader dilemma portfolio. The attraction of cost saving to the outsourcing of a particular service is high but the leader must be able to manage the performance process and maintain relations with the supplier. Relationships need to be formed with external parties where corporate values are sold into staff who do not actually work directly for the company. This parallels them more with the core workforce and the service provided as an outsourced purchase is in keeping with the original workings, values, and vision of the company. All too often, such purchase can be task or need led with short-term cost dictating the path taken. Jobs get done but are often not contextualized within the corporate whole thus leaving a gap.

Temporary or purchased structures are important in affording a company this cost effective flexibility with outsourcing and seasonal structuring giving organizations the chance to change more readily in different environments. Rather than finance the salaries of a team of full-time HR individuals, for instance, some companies spread some of the general HR tasks into the line management portfolio and buy in the expertise when it is needed. This is possible with a number of functions and does have the benefit of being flexible and up to date as well as saving on costs. The cascade of some of the duties into the jurisdictional arena of the different level leaders does also mean a more rounded understanding of the issues and a more rounded development for them in dealing with them. The counter argument here is that temporary/flexible options can lack particular obligation to the company and lack the accrued expertise which comes with having an intimate and historical knowledge of the company. Shipping in talent or service *pro rata necessitum* seems logical to enable a flexible approach but if the wider obligation, experience, and willingness is not there, a gap still exists in knowledgeable provision and corporate commitment which may be worse than the original lack of flexibility in the first place. It can also mean a series of different people looking after the needs of the organization leading to inconsistency and other inefficiencies because of communication problems. Such outsourced services will be more detached from the rhythm of the usual business so inevitably miss opportunities for linking events to other things or predicting or preventing possible future issues which may have been spotted by those *in situ*.

As well as outsourcing functions, organizations often outsource whole sections of the workforce to cope with seasonal fluctuations or to expand more safely in periods of growth. This renders a complete flexibility and gains the manpower without the long-term commitment. Being able to contract and expand according to demand and situation increases the speed of reaction to the market and is then held to increase competitive advantage. This may be the case in the short term where fast reactions are necessary but there are disadvantages with outsourcing parts of the workforce over longer periods of time. A "temporary" workforce is never going to be as committed as a permanent one and without the history and experience of the company, each temporary individual is less equipped to see the whole picture and tends to remain task driven. This could manifest itself in terms of a poorer quality of service or a lack of product knowledge. The end user/customer will feel the difference and may vote with their feet particularly if this is also accompanied by ever-changing people serving their needs.

The cost benefits to the business may outweigh these factors but that is the balance argument for the leader. There are disadvantages either way, so it is for the great leader to anticipate these and pre-empt their strike thus making their ultimate decision more likely to succeed.

It helps if the leader assesses the core and critical reasons for outsourcing. Often the decision to outsource is made for cost reasons, to reserve or conserve critical resources at the heart of the business and indeed increase the efficiency of resources across the board. Leaders have to decide what the core activities are in the company they wish to retain and what noncore or sometimes core activities they wish to trust in the hands of a partner organization. This can be difficult as on occasions, it may be best to outsource to gain expertise and on others it may be best to simply outsource more laborious and systematic parts of the processes.

Whatever the reasons for doing so, outsourcing is a key strategic tool and supports the strategic planning process. Whether driven by new technology, the economy, geographical penetration, legal, or cost factors outsourcing plays an important part in securing competitive advantage.

It is not approached lightly and it is important that the leader sets about it correctly. Value has to be identified and the process lined up with corporate strategy. Add to that the need to implement it correctly even once you have decided it is a necessity and there is plenty of room for error. Needless to say that there evolves a new communications role with such implementation. There will be a need to work across the organization after deciding this is the right way forward and another factor to consider is timing for best effect.

The leadership role is crucial for best use of such strategic tools and fully aware of the benefits, and of course the disadvantages, the leader can ensure the organization is ready for it to happen, facilitate integration of partners, ensure full value is realized, and communicated through the system and treat outsourcing as a whole process or project which needs full attention and management from start to finish.

Outer globalization

Outer globalization and the remote management pressures that will inevitably bring are major concerns for the modern leader in finding ways through. These areas cannot be completely covered in detail in this text but are worthy of important note as they are further and very large areas of deliberation for the great leader.

With the inside of the organization resilient and adaptable to its best ability, the whole enterprise is better placed to face the changes in its external environment. Outer globalization is the state of readiness of the organization for that environment as well as the actual effects of national and international expansion and easier communication over distance. Indeed, this is now a given and all organizations are subject to these influences. They are so subject to these external, economic, political, social, and technological influences now that the previous safety of local or national operation only subject to the economic influence of one country has disappeared. All operations whether multisited or not, whether international or not, are influenced by the global causal effect. Economic changes in one country now heavily influence trading in others more potently than before.

The term globalization itself can be confusing too when looking externally. On the one hand, as above, it is held that it is a positive access and communication of all cultures embracing their diversity and maximizing on the differences. On the other hand, some may view it as an invasion of one type of capitalism through countries starting to benefit from economic growth. China is the largest growing economy in present times and India is also a very fast growing economy following the technological changes which have brought companies the ability to access these huge markets for their buyers and suppliers. Globalization is no longer only something the affluent countries benefit from. Those in the developing countries may at first be the providers to the affluent purchasers in the world markets but in turn will become more affluent and be purchasers themselves creating an erratic and ever-changing global demand. The population growth in China and India has in itself become a global currency. The demographic power has attracted work from other countries and given that population a disposable income that they did not have before. Add technological advance and the effect is a more unified way forward. Political changes can also have similar outcomes as with Russia. The emerging oligarchs have their global impact too. Also networks and alliances can be formed by those who may not have considered it before when distance was actually a problem. Indeed, as the pressures of the global market increase and impact on profits, it is inevitable that more consolidation may occur in organizations as they feel they need to "size up" to the job. Mergers and acquisitions between companies further afield than before will bring the leader cultural and logistical challenges.

Therefore, the great leader will take their followers and the organization on a number of global expeditions to meet the milestones of the corporate strategic direction. The lucrative logistics of the globalization fast upon us means that suppliers can come from further afield and that services and production can be sited in other countries because quite simply it is cost effective. This gives an extra dynamic to the leadership in that not only does it include the strategic direction of the central operation but also a tightening and controlling of the communication links and activities of all the satellite services and operations – however, far afield they are in their new virtual status.

Remote management

Different leadership decisions are being made as we experience the repercussions of moving with the times and use the more sophisticated communications media. The money saved by changing supplier or moving production or service to another country is a bonus supported by the ease of electronic communication and this can give the company a clear advantage which can be passed on to the customer and so potentially increase market share and competitive standing.

On the other hand though, the same move can present new issues for leadership solution. Cultural conflicts may occur as may service delays or misunderstanding because the customer service is so far removed from the customer themselves. The customer may feel uncomfortable with a less personal service and solution to their needs. Interestingly, recent well-known advertising campaigns seem to reflect unique selling points pivoting on "locality" of service with a return to nearby supply or service you can "touch" rather than press a number of numbers on the telephone key pad to only then be processed rather than pacified. Of further interest is that this does not deny that "internationality" still is the main driver and that globalization is here to stay. It is the way leaders are learning to handle it that is changing not the fact that globalization reduces.

New skills of leadership are evolving and will further evolve. The successful remote management of more extended and convoluted set ups which have themselves evolved with the globalization is now more necessary. As organizations develop in this way it will be necessary to isolate the further skills leaders will need to keep things in line with the vision.

Although we are learning as things happen, there are common factors for consideration. The simple fact is that however complicated the virtual or actual structure of an organization is leadership contact with their followers changes considerably with outer globalization. Basically, the leader is physically further removed from the front line and also often the next in line so they have to communicate either through a longer chain of others or through alternative media. This being the case, the great leader must differentiate themselves from those who reactively cope and get by in the way they approach this challenge.

Without face-to-face reaction the leader is less able to use some of the personal attributes that make them that bit more special. They are robbed of the opportunity to impress their true character and personality on an individual or situation and must think carefully how to translate this through other people or through other media. What may be naturally delivered straight from the horse's mouth now needs detailed and thorough specification if delivered through another so that one can be as sure as possible that the right message will be transferred to the intended recipient. Then, there is the matter of trusting the messenger which brings a spotlight on their recruitment and development in the first place. And what if they are inherited? The complications which could occur are worrying. The only approach is for the leader to anticipate as many possible issues as they can and do everything they can to cater for their avoidance. It is clear that in a situation such as this the leader should be geared up for error prevention to avoid the time-consuming exercise of damage limitation later.

Where another person is not involved and one is reliant on media such as e-mail, and this is more and more common, even more diverted accommodations need to be considered. The leader must consider how they can extend their personality and motivational skills through this form which is not an easy task. A "ra ra ra" in group e-mail form can be useful but only has a fraction of the impact of a personal performance pushing the troops. In addition to this, the leader cannot see the reaction of the recipients to be able to judge whether the pitch is at the right level. Mind you, many a less than great leader has managed to misjudge that even with their staff right in front of them!

In addition to the tactical trip ups of remote management there are extra pressures at more strategic levels. Each time a new turn is needed in the component parts of the strategic plan, the great leader must mechanically and in some detail work out the repercussional effects of that turn up and down the line – not just in process terms but in emotional ones too. Beyond the mere two-dimensional effect, the leader must also think in three-dimensional satellite terms so that all aspects of the business, actual and virtual, are considered in the whole equation. It is easy, and fairly common, to overlook the impact of things on virtual or remote set ups and these oversights can be costly and cause more great delay. Time taken to think things through beforehand can be a real blessing in terms of saving costly mistakes.

Even once this is all thought through with the appropriate level of detail there is still the issue of its communication and again it is not just about getting across the actual instruction. There is so much more to consider and so many areas for retranslation when a remote situation applies.

The leader must think through what extra areas for extra emphasis are needed so the final message is of the right strength once it arrives at its destination. Add to this, the extra dynamic of considering the different abilities and agendas of the different people as well as the different media likely to be used to transport the message, not to mention the different cultural contexts, and a whole process of damage limitation occurs on top of the original leadership task. Not all potential blocks and issues can be predicted, it would be naïve to think so, but it is possible to greatly reduce the problems by investing time and deeper thought to the actual mechanics and meaning so the message at different levels and in different countries impacts in the desired way.

Remote management can be daunting but it cannot be avoided as it is becoming more than a likely task for today's great leader and another dimension for them to think in and through. This text cannot possibly do justice to this whole topic as it is really a whole study and text in itself. Where the time in this book has been devoted to collating and discussing a portfolio of leadership skills which either singly or combined give a 360 degree approach to taking the business forward from within, a further area outside for devotion has been isolated for further thought in terms of globalization and the remote management and leadership approach needed to approach it.

Internal relationships

Relationships inwards come down to levels of responsibility set out from the start. How much devolution occurs from the original ideas and instructions and who is involved in effecting them at the front line. The great leader not only works out the who but also the how each level/layer is kept motivated, communicated with, and aligned with the overall cause.

Delegation of particular tasks to individuals, units, divisions of the organization must all make up a whole picture from their individual contributions. First deciding what each task type and level should be is an important part of the leader's role, but also then monitoring it and aligning it with the overall direction. The master plan is now blueprinted at strategic business unit level and translated into their language. Further, this needs translating into financial allocations, targets, performance appraisals, and so on. Each unit needs to be liaised with carefully but then they need pulling together so each communicates with the other and duplication, error, and so on is avoided.

Processes, communications, and controls

Flow in and out of the business needs planning, efficient processes, and control. All must be aligned to the overall objectives and vision and in turn aligned at a different level with the structures set up to sustain them. Therefore, output targets or expectations are set. These must be aimed for and the effort of that aim monitored and motivated so this input toward it is appropriate to the set direction and not just habitual, directionless routine. In addition to deciding what has to be done, the question of who has the responsibility for it arises in terms of whether it is a directive from the top or whether the responsibility is delegated at a lower level in more indirect fashion. Either way, this too needs to be controlled and monitored. Top-down performance goals need bottom-up planning in terms of materials, human resources, time, systems, and standardizations. Synchronization of these processes and the people powering them is a sophisticated and demanding task.

The operationalization of the vision is now starting to take place. Performance indicators are set and review/control processes considered and implemented. Further, the great leader must consider how information is disseminated within and without the organization. The speed and effectiveness of the communications will be essential to supporting the structure designed and the processes surrounding it. The detail of communication cascade will be dealt with in the next few chapters but for this purpose, it is important to note its power on the hard and soft structural make up of the operational aspects of the organization. For instance – it would only take one not so obliging line manager to retranslate the vision in their own way to block an efficient communication system. The great leader must evaluate the passage of information through, around, and up and down the organization looking for such potential barriers and ensuring a smooth run every way possible. Cascade time from Boardroom to front line is a classic issue as is ensuring that information can actually get back up the other way from the front line to the Board room.

Add to this the increasing communication issues associated with more remote management as organizations structure in more diversified ways and decentralize or part decentralize their operations. Cascade time is one issue but so then is effect – the lack of direct effect that is. The great leader then has to produce communication systems which support this structural set up and allow for speed and translation across many sites as well as many levels in today's global structures. This will be discussed further in the concluding chapter.

With more pick up points, there are fewer places to hide too. Ethical conduct can be inspected as well as encouraged from the heart of the conscience of the company. The ethical conduct of the leader is also more transparent this way so, equally, there is a security in knowing that internal controls keep check on progress and also of course help that progress be recognized and attributed to the correct, hardworking individuals. It works both ways for the benefit of the leader in terms of their control and for the benefit of the workforce in that they know where they stand and where they will be recognized. Further, the reassurance that all is on track in terms of the strategic direction, renders a greater confidence in the enterprise from its internal customers so stakeholder value stays high and the leadership stock market is less of a lottery.

Ethical edification

The mortar for the structural design of the company is made in part by its ethical conduct and standing. The moral disposition of the company and each of its individuals will not only dictate the necessary structural design of internal and external systems and processes but also hold it together – or not.

This mortar is multilevel. From the corporate stand on moral ground such as corporate social responsibility, to the lack of hypocrisy in the leadership in that they have the same standards for themselves as well as for their staff, to each individual's personal corporate conduct, and how their sense of duty links to the overall belief of the company.

The theological approach of the company with the ethical stance that it is the consequences or outcome of all actions which judges the level of ethicality might also conflict with the deontological approach which starts with the rights of the individual whose ethics pivot on freedom. Therefore the leader may face conflict then between making a decision because it was right in individual human terms and the consequences of not doing so which may endanger staff in the future, and making a decision because the science of the spreadsheet allows for it as it is the most effective and efficient way for the majority.

With such potential conflict between mission and motive at many levels, the leader must work a balance of thinking involving both and so deduce the best solution from an evenly weighted evaluation to find ways through.

If only it were that simple. Strategic, structural, and systems decisions are not only dependant on the debate between individual and overall rights at the time as discussed above but also between the long-term interests of the individual – egoism – and the long-term interests of the involved or wider community – utilitarianism.

This then brings forward the thought of how leaders know what is right for the greater good or what is best for the long-term interests of one of their staff. Even then there is the complication that a utilitarian approach is itself divided between act and rule. The act approach goes for that greater good despite the rules and the rules approach means that all decisions are made within a prescribed set of rules.

The rigid structure of the rules safety net is somewhat softened by their disregard for a greater cause – or the view that the end justifies the means.

Case study comment

Role pressures and limitations

"... inspectors, in my philosophy, are there to give us as objective a picture as they can on the basis of professional activity. If they cannot see everything they should report that. They should report their own limitations. We never said that there were no weapons of mass destruction. We said that in the course of 700 inspections, we haven't seen any and that we have been all over the place and been with the people on the sites. We said we have been to sites that were given to us as tips by intelligence and we did not find any weapons of mass destruction. So, you could suspect there was something wrong about their sources, since they tipped us about sites that were empty of weapons of mass destruction. We reported our skepticism about the intelligence but we also said that we could not check everything in a big country. There were many caves and basements ... We did know the country well from the 1990's but it's a big place and hiding a prototype of a centrifuge or hiding some biological substance – it doesn't take much space. So, we did not go further in our conclusions than our material allowed. That's my objection to Scott Ritter, who overstates his case to bring support to a political line of action. We

▶

said no, that's not our role. The Security Council has the political power and we are its servants. What do international civil servants do? We dig up, compile and serve the facts as best we can. We leave it to the Council to decide."

Hans Blix, responsible for UN weapons inspections in Iraq

The great leader finds ways through by safeguarding the basic framework of the rules toward the end goal but seeing the impact at all levels to evaluate whether they need to evolve for the greater good. This all sounds very moralistic and aimed at the ideal world, but there is a territory we have not yet explored and that is the ethical core of the leader themselves.

The individual interests of the leader can often conflict with the overall and greater good of the company. Many top-level executives have a short time to prove themselves so it could be suggested that their actions are not necessarily in the greater interests of that company – but in ensuring that they stay in their job and make the greatest short-term impact on the Chair. This provides another thought tangent for consideration. Some leaders may use a utilitarian cover and even perhaps present a convincing argument for it. It may not actually be the right argument for corporate good but will help the short-term plight of that person in office at the time.

Danni Jost examines the principles for retaining a high ethical stance.

Case study comment

Personal principles

"This is what I try to apply in my own life with various degrees of success. In what follows I am inspired from what I have learned as an Aikido student (Aikidoka). It is based on the code of the now defunct cast of Japanese Samurai about which much romanticized folklore abounds in the West. There is actually very little that is romantic about the way of life of the Samurai, or let's say it is as romantic as the life of a monk. It was a way of life, from what I glean from it, that required incredible amounts of discipline and the cultivation of a strict honour code. Modern day Japanese, for the most part, may think that this is all rather quaint, and certainly very old fashioned.

However your working title for your book immediately made me think of the fact that there are seven virtues that a Samurai cultivates throughout life. These seven virtues (or values) are represented in the seven pleats of an hakama, the traditional outer skirt that a Samurai wore. Today the hakama is still part of traditional formal dress and can be worn by both men or women.

So here are those values that use in my life, in no particular order:

1. Courtesy

2. Honour

3. Integrity

4. Honesty

5. Benevolence

6. Loyalty

7. Courage"

Dannie Jost – Executive Leadership Consultant

Walk the talk

Look for ethical conflicts/dilemmas at different levels in your organization. Taking one per day, put aside 15 minutes

▶

to quickly balance out how appropriate current approaches are in handling it.

Take a moment to think through whether all of your actions are made with the company in mind. Be honest with yourself – are there and have there been occasions where self-interest has influenced your direction?

If we presume that the leader is acting in the best interests of the company and not themselves, then there are still areas they must examine to find the fairest way through. The repercussional effect of their decisions should be borne in mind from the start and as they seek the right way through that particular context and circumstance, then it is also wise to set aside thinking time for the impact that decision will make on others. What might seem like the right and moral approach may affect others in a negative way and be at their expense.

For instance, if an organization decides to implement a reward strategy where office bonuses are equally shared between all staff, this would seem to be an ethical approach with the good of all in mind. In practice however, discord occurs as those who work harder than others do feel they are at an individual disadvantage and proceed to resent the "lazier" individuals as well as the corporate ethical stance. Rules can often be made to restrict the actions of the few who may take advantage of a situation. These then penalize those who would not stretch the ethical boundaries. It seems that there is no clear win. Finding ways forward through softer ethical means has its own hard lessons to be learned. A relative approach where a hybrid of the two is a natural default for the leader will avoid the dangers of absolutism. The leader must then consistently ensure they maintain a system for balancing the two.

Walk the talk

Are there areas in your organization where ethical intentions have been good but it may have backfired in accidentally

discriminating a party you had not thought of? How could
this been reevaluated and have you a system of walking the
idea through to check the impact on the stakeholders?

Finding ways through moral dilemmas

Making these ethical decisions involves weighing up the moral
dilemmas between making the company as successful as possible
or meeting strict targets and looking after the interests of the staff
and the public concerned. Decisions between short-term and
long-term obligations of the individual and the many are further
pressed upon by corporate need over the short term and the long
term (Figure 4.1). This creates situations where even the most
honest leader can be tempted to act according to the route of least
resistance rather than the most appropriate way forward.

Case study comment

Handling the paradox

"There are however a few semantic nuggets packed in my
thesis that being human has something to do with the need
to balance paradoxes. What do I mean by being human?
Let me try to make this clear.

To be human to me is to be open to what our individual
and social development potential is. I realize that this may
be a different way of defining humanity than what is more
commonly accepted in learned circles. I am of the view
that we – humans – as a species are continually evolving
and one key to that evolution is through the development
of our inner capabilities that include the individual's intel-
lect and spiritual self together with collective behaviours
(culture). This is what I would call my fundamental
Menschenbild (idea of man) and the core reference point

▶

in my own thinking about what concerns human behaviours and experience.

Although transhumanism is one of the disciplines in which I engage, I do not subscribe to the idea that humans need technological correction in an hardware sense for their undesired and unnecessary behaviours. To me to imagine an ideal and utopian world populated by equally ideal and optimized creatures, is to imagine boredom incarnated, and the perfect scenario for doomsday. Nothing kills humanity faster than boredom. Life needs challenge.

In other words to be human is to be lacking against the theoretical perfection. What makes the species remarkable is its ability to deal with the lacks, the imperfections, and the conflict and tension that this creates. It is exactly this imperfection of the species and its social aggregate that create the so called paradoxes. Paradoxes are inherent to the human condition. To claim that paradoxes are not good and to fight them with all means is to me tantamount to being in a state of denial.

So, a wise CEO will have in his or her skill set the ability to balance paradoxes both at the personal level, but also at the organisational level. This is however a skill that is not often, if ever, taught in grammar school or later at university. It is a skill that is learnt either through the caretaker's nurturance or one that is learnt through experience, and very often it is learnt at an unconscient (or intuitive) level. The bottom line for me here is that this is a skill that can be learned, and that it is the individual's choice to make how much inner strength (spirit) he or she wants to develop.

This is easy to understand if one draws the parallel between body and spirit. To me those are related and intimately interconnected as the fabric's mesh of what makes up a human being. At the physical body level we vary from one end of the spectrum as obese couch potatoes to well

▶

tuned vibrant svelte athletes. This points us to the fact that our bodies are rather adaptable and capable of learning. The difference between the couch potato and the athlete is the amount of discipline and training that has been focused on developing or not developing the body and its responses. The same goes with the inner spirit inhabiting the body."

Dannie Jost – Executive Leadership Consultant

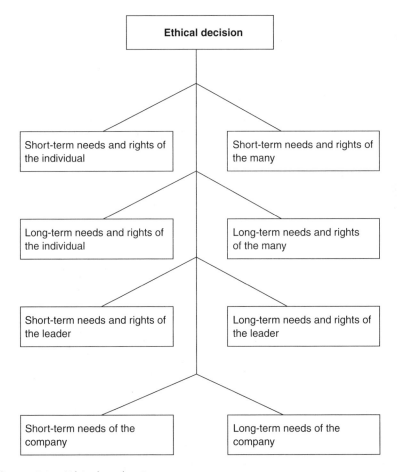

Figure 4.1   Ethical evaluation

Source: Compiled by authors

All of these factors then have a knock on effect on the others showing that there are links to be considered and even a moral cycle. Short-term corporate need may set short-term deadlines of some significance for the leader. Decisions on how these targets are met will be made perhaps over and above the consideration of long-term effect or impact on the stakeholding individuals. In addition to a knock on effect there is also a knock across effect when one considers the inclusion of those in the supply chain. There will be a number of ethical considerations and dilemmas when facing the pressure of speed and cost of supply to the organization and conflicts of interest will occur at many levels of the structural framework and the chain attached to it.

When shareholders demand profit and success, when other competing companies perhaps adopt more corrupt practices rather than lose the business, the leader is in a corner. Choices have to be made between cost and caring. There is no one solution as each situation varies so much but one common denominator in achieving success must be the clear communication and honesty of the leader themselves. If it is clear what pressures are on them and the organization, staff will be more able to assist with the best ethical compromise possible or indeed be able to underpin sticking it out on the highest moral ground possible. They may also understand more if shareholder pressures upset investment within.

It need not be a simple clash of need as above. The leader could also be sandwiched between two very and equally important moral positions which conflict. Here it is essential to furnish the correct neutrality to both parties and mediate their causes while lining them up with the strategic direction of the organization.

Decisions on how these are met can also be heavily reliant on any incentive/bonus the leader may be tempted with to achieve them. Even less innocent than this is the possibility that some leaders may be tempted into less honest means to achieve their goal and keep their job. Drilling further down then, it is evident that there are further convolutions to the theme. How the leader judges what incentives or if you like "bribes" to accept as the norm or proper must be down to the individual integrity of that person. It is clear that the individual ethical standing of the leaders themselves is pivotal to properly conducted progress.

It does not stop there as practices will be emulated or considered as a cultural norm. The ethical example set by the leader is key to maintaining the moral way forward or not. *Contract by conduct* is easily bedded into the corporate culture if everyone enters a "groupthink" approach. Fiddling expenses, helping yourself to the contents of the stationery cupboard, surfing the internet on company time, and so on can all be justified as, "well everyone else does it so it is ok!" It begs the question as to what is worse, the repeated petty crime over time, or the one-off but very much regretted enticement into temptation.

Communication systems have a hand in the corporate ethical cartilage too. The hard structural impact of this will be looked at later in the chapter but the soft systems which are borne of individual and corporate ethical interest are indeed interesting in themselves. What information is allowed to flow freely and what is contained is another matter for debate and another area for ethical dilemma. What level of privacy should be decided upon compared to what levels of transparency should be practiced is hard to decide.

In all, there is a plethora of possibilities for the unethical enthusiast! The ethical player then can look at these issues in four ways:

1. It is actually naïve to think all unethical behavior can be eradicated from a company and one should aim for the best possible clean up by creating hard and soft structures which make as much as possible transparent.
2. Ethical behavior is entirely dependent on the leader and their line managers in terms of their beliefs and practices.
3. Rules and codes of ethics do need to be formed and applied to provide a structure within which to work and judge situations.
4. The norms set by the company itself in terms of its standards of acceptance are evaluated to ensure that corporate culture does not norm staff into unethical behavior through practices or pressures.

Within all this, and indeed without this, then there is the matter of cultural underpinning and envelopment. Value differences in different cultures, corporate as well as national, will influence what is acceptable or not.

Having managed all of this, the leader then needs to think laterally about how this manifests itself up and down and across the supply chain. Careful consideration around practices is necessary especially at third- and fourth-level supplier. These parties need to be won over to ensure that they practice in line with the central company and follow their CSR practices. It may even be necessary to educate and advise these suppliers how this needs to be done. Standards not only need to be set but agreed and then monitoring with a series of internal controls will be a key barometer as to whether they are adhered to. It is through the quality of these relationships, understandings, and working practices between the parent company and the different levels of suppliers, the clearly drafted legal expectations and agreements and the application of systematic controls and procedures for decision making that a uniformity of quality is achieved.

This is not to say that these relationships are easy to develop and maintain. Frankly, it is difficult to get third-party suppliers to buy into all ethical dimensions of the parent company. Cost drivers will always influence ethical actions from those further away from the heart of the company so it takes a very determined organization indeed to ensure that these relationships are pulled in tighter. This is necessary to buffer the cost driven nature of such supply and involves not just forming close relationships where a holistic bond may make the difference but also implementing efficient and disciplined systems of control over what is and is not acceptable.

This pulls the suppliers in the right directions toward the vision too and prevents potential errors and bottlenecks which could hold up progress.

The cultural carriageway

Intertwined throughout this soft structural security is the semi-visible matter of culture.

Starting from the top, the company can be accused of creating culture which may encourage unethical behavior. Targets, bonuses, pressure in the Boardroom may all contribute to what decisions are made and how and therefore what practices become the corporate norm. Indeed, it should be said there is a Boardroom *subculture* and this in its turn will affect the flavor of the rest of the company. External factors such as the economy or consumer purchasing patterns may press the company into having to evolve a certain culture to gain the competitive advantage. The presence or not of competitors will also have an effect on how the company must react and this will have an effect on the climate within the company.

If culture is the total of the shared beliefs and values that the organizational staff hold and practice then these can be, and are, affected in many ways.

Aside from those suggested above where pressure is powered and cascaded from the top down, there are many other directions this soft structure is impacted by and the leader must ponder on what is affected and where from.

Hard structures cannot be suddenly changed or formed without consideration of the soft structures which already exist. They are in existence for a reason and before the leader sits down to change corporate hierarchies and form certain communication links, it is imperative to respect the influences of these semi-visible structures.

In addition to establishing the cultural norms influenced from inside and out, the leader should take into account their organic nature. Once isolated, it is important to note that they are likely to evolve so the cultural balance sheet approach needs the support of a *cultural cash flow forecast* to make it robust enough for decision making. The cultural carriageway stretches from the original founder to the desired or likely future of the organization. It is then also carved toward that future by the fellows within (Figure 4.2).

Figure 4.2   The cultural carriageway

Source: Compiled by authors

Founder

All cultural journeys must start with the original founder of the organizations. They would have set up the company based on their values and beliefs and put their heart and soul into the enterprise and its success. As well as providing the purpose, they will also be part of that purpose themselves.

Fellows

The believers in the company and its founder, or "founder fellows," are the first wave of cultural embedding. Followers of the original vision will form a strong bond. That is not to say that there will not be cultural differences and beliefs within as anywhere, just that it is more likely that at this stage there is a greater uniformity of belief in the overall.

Such a soft structure of "founder fellows" will impact beyond any hard structure designed by the leader. This base will flavor the company for evermore even after takeovers, mergers, and so on. Even after they are long gone, the ghost of the original entity will remain.

The acceptance of this is a start and the realization that those former fellows were of great value to the position reached today will be an added bonus. All too often the easier and perhaps less intellectual route is to bad mouth the past and its beliefs – but they are what after all brought us to the present time. Things may need to change but not by deriding corporate history. It is and will stay a part of the corporate culture.

Fellows will of course evolve with incremental cultural progression, that of the company and that they have a need for within themselves. The leader should take into account that this will be at different levels and at different speeds and a cultural change plan will need to be considered to accommodate the diversity.

Future

It cannot escape. Change for competitive advantage is a necessity and future visions will inevitably be different to some of those held in the past. At the same time as holding the foundations strong the leader needs to anticipate likely changes in the economy, demographic buying patterns, and so on. rather than sit and wait for them to hit hard suddenly. It will be necessary to change attitudes within and consider the embedded history which has evolved as the corporate culture. Part of that culture for the future is how change will be tackled and how the leader channels the company for that change.

To achieve progress toward channeling cultural change, a look at the likely covert practices in existence is a good tip. The subterranean practices and attitudes alluded to in the previous chapter need to be uncovered or at least guessed at in the best possible way by the leader. This way channeling change will be more of an accurate science – not that it can ever be exact. With stiff competition at the ready to benefit from any internal vulnerability, it is also necessary to consider working to a time limit and clock progress (Figure 4.3).

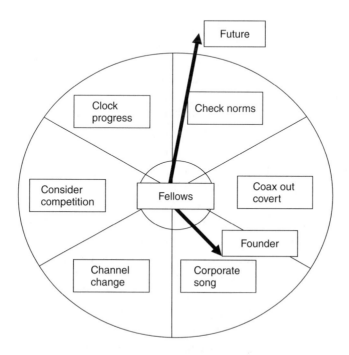

Figure 4.3   The cultural clock

Source: Compiled by authors

Therefore, the cultural carriageway of Founder, Fellows, and Future above includes some key factors within

- checking the norms
- coaxing out the covert
- corporate song
- channeling change
- consider competition
- clock progress

Walk the talk

Work around the cultural clock and apply it to your situation. For, each element creates two actions which may make a difference to this valuable soft structure.

Picking up on the previously but briefly mentioned Board room subculture, it is necessary to acknowledge the impact from this source on the cultural clock above. The "Board" will have a culture of its own and it is perhaps a good idea to consider this subculture as a subdivision of "Fellows." Here we are talking about the senior fellows. Their bond, history, ability, agreement levels, personalities, routines, structure, and so on will all impress upon the whole organization in many ways. Such an influencing party could be a cohesive extension of the organization where all sing the company song and whatever disagreements naturally occur in the normal course of the *Boardroom Bash*, all support the one agreed line of action for the good of the whole in a synergic fashion. At the opposite end of the scale, and as discussed in previous chapters, there may be a split in the ranks causing internal conflict and the need for a survivalist reaction. In between, there may be a supportive approach from the Board where issues are discussed at source and communications are open in addition to a strategist culture where development toward the future is the overriding focus. Baroness Jones spotted this issue when taking on the Chair at Shelter. Gaining clarity of roles to start off the Board bonding process was her stop.

> **Case study comment**
>
> Clarity in the Committee
>
> "We now have Terms of Reference of all the Committees. We know what the roles of the board members are. We know what the role of the Executive is. We know what the role of the new Chairman we recruit is going to be. We just documented everything at that very, very basic level. So we've done that and we've also spent some time on a week-end away looking at relationships between the Board and the Executive which were not good, they were pretty strained, and still not perfect, but we are beginning to understand each other a lot better than we have done."
>
> Baroness Maggie Jones, Trustee of Shelter

Whether, synergic, survivalist, supportive or strategist in nature, the Board culture will cascade and be copied in the various subhierarchies which exist in the company.

These too may then have a subculture of their own. Some may not mimic the Board's influence and continue in their own pattern. This may conflict with the overall culture and cause problems.

However great the leader it is impossible to cover every one of these angles. What is important is to realize their existence so as many avenues are covered as possible. Looking for softer structures and indeed helping create the right ones will ensure that hard structural design is all the more successful.

Conclusion

Finding ways forward from the original vision base incorporates a blend of hard and soft approaches to hard and soft structures which already exist within the organization or which should exist within the organization. The vectorization of the vision is a complicated matter and needs to be tackled with a 360 degree sensitivity again pinpointing potential conflicts to save, or rather focus more positively, corporate energy. As this materializes, dilemmas will present themselves in terms of ethics and culture – the soft structural make up of the organization. The great leader needs to ensure these soft mechanisms are acknowledged and incorporated into any hard structural design plans stemming from their strategic choice and then further drill down into responsibility and communication cascade levels to ensure a whole framework is created where each plane compliments the other rather than aggravates it. This all then needs to be contextualized into the bigger picture as global pressures arise and more direct influence is diluted with the more indirect skills of remote management.

Great rate

This chapter has touched on some of the elements of "finding ways forward." It is not a definitive list but the elements which seem to make the difference involve:

Vision Vectors

Ethical Edification

Cultural Clock

Mission Milestones

Ethical Evaluation

Contract by Conduct

Subculture

Cultural Carriageway

Cultural Cash Flow Forecast

Boardroom Bash

Strategic Choice

Structural Design

History and Mystery Shopping

Strategic Alignment

CHAPTER 5

Engaging

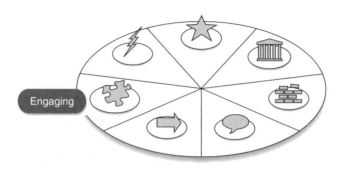

Source: Compiled by authors

Chapter introduction

Effective engaging
Gaining the willing effort and buy in from the employee

Buy in
Gaining an emotional commitment from the workforce

Delegation and empowerment
Allocating tasks and responsibilities which develop staff and
which ensure a sense of achievement, ownership, and pride

Communication channels
Clearing ways for the movement of information and identifying potential blocks and misunderstandings before they
happen

Polylogue
Multiple dialogue which has open and free voice for shared and more effective decision making

As we drill down through systems and sentiments to find great leadership anchor points for more stable success, a level of extra commitment from the workforce becomes evident. It is available to the right leader with the right skills and must be sought out and thought out carefully.

Once the individual and the team needs have been identified by the leader to extract that extra output from each unit, there is an extra level beyond that obvious synergy. This is where true empowerment is, given the room and where real ownership occurs. This is where a true and long-term bond is created between the individual and the organization and where that extra willing effort is truly given freely.

This does not happen by accident and the correct conditions must be cultivated to allow the room for it to thrive. As well as clear translation of the vision into its component parts at the different levels, there is a need for the right level of fluidity of communication as well as the allowance for more intimate and personal communication. This will have been considered when designing structures and systems as previously mentioned but to really effect their presence a little more work is needed.

As well as knowing what to do, why and where that effort fits into the bigger picture, employees also need to feel part of the decision-making process. Not in a token way but in a real way which, they can see, is part of the operation for good. They are after all the front-line experts and can give the precise advice needed for increased success.

Only with the allowance of this input and a degree of decision level and practical autonomy will come a bond of responsibility and accountability. A good environment for free dialogue or even multilogue or perhaps polylogue where information is truly in freeflow and transparent in nature will break down "them and us" barriers, creates a more satisfied workforce, and a higher respect for the great leader who earns that respect rather than commands it.

All of this will involve further leadership skill in terms of how to present material and how to communicate effectively with a diverse workforce. Detailed consideration of the presentation packages and their impact will make the difference between forcing out compliance and cultivating alliance. This is where leaders really get staff to work because the staff want to – not because they have to. This is the true creation of desire within the workforce to enable them and their work output to be more than a completed task but an integral, essential, and organic part of the whole organization and its success.

Walk the talk

Think back on the last ten times staff have presented you with a completed task/request.

Now choose which of these applied to each of the individual situations.

1. Completed with enthusiasm and perhaps even more than what asked for
2. Completed as per instruction with only information asked for
3. Completed late or needed a lot of chasing and information given reluctantly

   1 = Effective
   2 = Efficient
   3 = Are you in the right job?

With a quick back of an envelope calculation, evaluate your percentages of the three.

Effective engaging

To gain an employee's true involvement, and it is attraction not force which will achieve it, the great leader must achieve a "buy in" from them at an emotional and very human level. Getting someone to do something transactionally is relatively easy and involves no real leadership ability at all. However, this just gets a job done and does not bring contextualization, heart, feeling, understanding, ownership, pride, commitment, and so on into the equation at all. Engagement involves a human and empathic approach from the leader to extract a human and emotionally committed approach from the follower.

Some leaders may despair at yet another drive toward the "touchy, feely" elements which seem periodically in fashion. It should be made clear that it is not an alternative approach to the others but an additional skill to gain additional support from the followers. It is not a fashion as the followers are human beings with their own feelings and all too often overly crisp job specifications, defined work areas, and departmental areaisations kill off the community spirit within a company. It would be fair to say that the more human aspects of great leadership have come more to the fore in recent years and would seem then to be a new fashion to some. Perhaps, though it is here to stay. Acknowledging the importance of employee input at all levels and injecting a certain equalism of respect toward all efforts within the corporate hierarchy is a positive and permanent result of our past mistakes.

Therefore, it is evident that while structure and systems are important in terms of the free flow of ideas and communication they furnish through the company, it is the skill of the leader not only in making this work that counts but also in gluing together the human component parts which will really breathe the life and longetivity into the organization. At this point, and in mind of the structural and systems designs in place, it is also necessary for the leader to consider the empathic abilities of their envoys. They will have a number of subleaders at different levels evangelizing the overall message with them but the whole thing could get blocked because of one stubborn "official" whose position is more important than the corporate direction. Although it would be great to think these leader types went out with the ark, it would be naïve to overlook the fact that all great leaders will have one or two of these in their hierarchies. Whatever "Uriah Heap" type noises they make at Board level, a different animal may emerge at ground level and the hard work and emotional investments put in elsewhere can be badly tainted by such approaches. It is also fair to say that every good move makes one-step forward but that every bad one makes several back.

The great leader is not only devising their own emotional approaches and responses but also that of their representatives.

Walk the talk

Stop and do a quick check that all your direct reports are communicating your message in the way you want.

Effective engagement then means the emotional and communicative abilities of the leader, of their direct reportees, of the reportees after that, and so on. It means ensuring their easy approachability as well as ensuring that they approach others in the right way. It means allowing room for the diversity of personalities within the teams they have and cultivating an environment of trust. It means allowing healthy debate to occur right through the ranks without discord or resent. It means ensuring that not only their door is open to the staff but also that staff open their doors to them. It is a balance of encouraging dialogue at multiple levels and a culture of respect for others and their opinions even if they are different.

Steven Crawshaw, CEO of Bradford and Bingley Plc suggests that this works across and upwards too.

Case study comment

Across the board

"The chairman I think was instrumental in giving me license to really talk to the board, to relay the brass tacks

▶

> about what needed to happen and the board were properly questioning of some fundamental decisions including decisions and numbers that had been round the table ... . I never had a moments back biting or bitching from any of them to be perfectly honest, they were wholly supportive and have continued to this day being wholly supportive, so I was very fortunate. But the route into that I think for a chief executive should always be through the chairman and doesn't matter how good the board is if the chairman is not doing his job properly, its very, very difficult for the chief executive and I have regularly blessed my chairman as a result of having made my 3 years as CEO a whole lot easier."
>
> Steven Crawshaw, CEO, Bradford and Bingley Plc

Buy in

Achieving buy in to a high degree would seem to involve a three-pronged attack by the leader in terms of them addressing their particular skills set. It would be essential to assess the levels of perception in oneself to admit what intelligence is present in terms of emotional understanding of others and perhaps even intuition. There is the thought that the more research a leader does on his staff in terms of their background, the "luckier" they get in terms of interpreting the thoughts and feelings of others. Perhaps *emotional commitment* does not have to be a natural talent and can be acquired through careful consideration and a bit of homework. More than surfacing sentiments though, this is anticipating them and really trying to get a grip on how the employee would feel in different situations. In addition to raising the awareness of feelings as discussed in previous chapters, there is a clear need to scenario plan those sentiments and make educated guesses as to the needs and wants of the individual. This "perception" or anticipation of need will impress the staff member and where things do go wrong, which inevitably they will from time to time, the leader is more easily forgiven as the intentions are good. This human move using the science of the head as well the caring from the heart will be rewarded in a real emotional commitment from those the leader has expressed such emotional commitment to.

This move, even if it has to be more engineered for the first few runs, will help secure the good will, the willing effort within and get the employees to really care about what they are doing. Rona Cant was asked how she thought this was achieved in her adventurous potential achieving experiences.

Case study comment

Purchasing passion

"I think what you have to do is get everybody to buy into the vision and to understand that they can do it and it is not impossible. There are strategies you can use but you all have to work together, because the power of one is less than the power of two/three or four. If you have several of you working together and helping each other you become a real team, and you put aside the fact that one is a leader. The leader has to be prepared to do the worst job. I don't think any leader can say 'I am the leader and I am not doing that!' No one is going to follow that sort of person and you really do have to get your hands dirty, your people have to understand that you know what they are going through. They have to know that you have been through it and that you can do what they are doing and that they can do what you are doing. You lead from the front and say 'come on guys we can do this.' And motivate them to actually achieve the goal."

How do you get them to buy into the vision and how do you motivate them?

Case study comment

"Well if you have a passion for the vision and you show them how it can be achieved and that it isn't impossible, I think then, you have more buy in. What is the benefit, ▶

what is the value? I did a talk for a pharmaceutical company and they wanted to know, how could they get people to buy more of their pills? My response was that you have to show them the benefits! You show them the value and the benefit of buying the pills. For instance, my Doctor told me I had a high cholesterol level, he said 'if you take these pills you are less likely to get a heart attack', so am I going to take the pills or not take the pills? Obviously I am going to take the pills; I don't want a heart attack. You have got to be passionate about the goal, that's a given. If you are passionate about the goal and you share with them what your goal is, what the vision is, what the passion is and you actually show them how it can be achieved and how it will help them to achieve the goal as well."

Rona Cant – Adventurer

Delegation and empowerment

Delegation and empowerment are the next item on the checklist for achieving buy in and true engagement (see Table 5.1). This follows on logically from the emotional levels just mentioned and the leader needs to look at the tasks in terms of their appropriate delegation. Task allocation and division will already have been decided at earlier stages but empowering the recipient with the true responsibility and the powers to achieve it are important parameters for the leader to set. The follower must have the appropriate amount of motivation and access to consultation with the leader as appropriate to their ability as well as clear guidelines as to exactly what needs doing and why.

Real empowerment as a result of a delegated task will involve a real sense of pride in the work by the employee. Not only should they be wholeheartedly bought into the experience but, if done properly, the experience should develop them and encourage them to use their own initiative. How often is it the case that delegated tasks are merely the boring ones no one wants to do and these get cascaded down the ranks causing the demotivation of those the tasks come to. Managers and leaders may be running

Table 5.1 Steps 1–8 on how to DELEGATE

1	D	Determine development opportunity
2	E	Evaluate the training need
3	L	Look for and check understanding
4	E	Empower and establish their commitment
5	G	Give support appropriate to the individual
6	A	Assess progress in a way suitable to them
7	T	Tell others it is happening and attribute any glory to them
8	E	Establish a positive delegating culture

around in overly busy fashion and be pushed to stress simply because they have not thought through the process of delegation and empowerment properly. They have more to do because they have not developed staff to take over. This may simply be fear. Leaders may be worried about a failed outcome and not trust the employee. However, if that employee is properly briefed and trained there is no excuse. It may be fear of not being in control but good delegation and effective empowerment is a higher-level demonstration of effective leadership control.

The leader really cannot lose as even if the task goes a bit wrong – a learning experience has been undergone and development for the better of the company and individual has taken place. The leader also develops their delegation skills further as they learn what to anticipate the next time. Not delegating effectively is denying the organization its growth. It is in effect an indirect corporate theft borne out of incompetence.

It may also be the case that there exists a greater expertise in the team itself so delegation to them actually strengthens the company and the value of the decisions made. Rona Cant experienced this on a round the world yacht race.

Case study comment

Purchasing passion – contd

"Sometimes as you go along you need to make changes to actually make the vision happen, you have to be flexible.

▶

When we were sailing round the World, our skipper was a brilliant sailor and understood the yacht perfectly but he had not had a lot of experience in ocean racing so we took a leaf out of Shackleton's book and made him more powerful by putting a mastermind group around him, he was still the skipper but he could make more knowledgeable decisions. No one can know everything and when you are racing the weather forecast is your route map, our weatherman really understood the weather, so we put him with the skipper. One of the Watch Leaders had done quite a lot of ocean racing and as he understood the intricacies of it we put him with the skipper. My watch leader was a Managing Director so we put him with the skipper as well as he was very good with people. Once we had this mastermind group around him, our performance improved because the crew had more confidence in the fact that more knowledgeable decisions were being made."

Rona Cant – Adventurer

Walk the talk

Take your last ten delegated tasks to your workforce and assess whether each falls into the "develop" category or the "dumped" category. If less than 75 percent of the tasks were development in nature, construct an action plan to rectify this within the next week.

D – Determine development opportunity

Rather than start with the desire to "dump" an unattractive task, it is more efficient to think through the opportunities that task brings before the leader. It may be easier to allocate a task to someone who has done it before and take the quickest or easiest route. However, what may seem to save time in the short term only steals it from the long term. By giving a range of duties to a range of staff, more expertise for the individuals concerned is cultivated and the company and the leader gain. This may take a little longer in the first instance but will save many more times this in later dividends. Such an approach involves the leader stopping and thinking at source. They must triage the tasks according to an overall gain and also to gain a greater level of satisfaction in the workforce. Choosing appropriate things for staff to do with their development in mind will pull the participating individual closer to the company as well as the leader.

With this in mind, at the higher levels of leadership it is necessary to think this through in a multilevel way so that subdelegation is considered and key influencing staff are trained to delegate effectively.

E – Evaluate the training need

Once the development opportunity has been isolated and the most appropriate individual chosen, the training they need to do the job must be assessed. This may be the introduction of a new skill or it may simply be a clear briefing. What is important is that the individual is set up with all the tools and skills necessary to do the job. If it is the first time they have done something, then the experience of the delegated task will be training in itself.

L – Look for and check understanding

Post evaluation of the training needs is necessary to look for the level of understanding. Not simply in terms of the technical elements of any task but in terms of the individual knowing where it fits in to the overall picture and how important it is to the company. The simple gaining of feedback can save a lot of time spent on a misunderstood task where the recipient has got the wrong end of the stick or the delegator has inadequately briefed in the necessary details. It is also essential to check the understanding of deadlines and exactly what they expect. This is the responsibility of the leader. If this is misunderstood then it is their poor perception that is at fault.

E – Empower and establish their commitment

In addition to a clear understanding and the skills and tools to do the job, it is also necessary to ensure the individual has the correct amount of power to get everything done they need. Leaders can misjudge the situation in terms of expecting a work-force to respond to others the way they would themselves. This is often not the case so it is important they also have the dele-gated authority to assert themselves in the right way. This trust will also firm up their commitment which should be checked again at this stage. In fact, the level of trust put in the individual will have a direct effect on the quality of their output. Commitment is often greatly increased where the individual feels they have been given that extra layer of trust or pushed to their higher developmental levels.

G – Give support appropriate to the individual

This level should be agreed according to the individuals' need and be positive in nature rather than criticizing things they do. The support should be available throughout the process and especially afterwards when they need to feed back how they felt they did.

A – Assess progress in a way suitable to them

Assessment or audit can take place with a support agreement in place. Good old-fashioned audit can be reframed in softer terms but obviously is important. The leader must have certain measures/objectives in mind so they can give the correct support but this needs to be done without offending or undermining the individual. Deciding on how assessments take place is also a mutual agreement between the two parties and must then be adhered to by both so there is the accountability but the individual still feels they are in control of the delegated task and that they still have the freedom to input in their own individual way too. An agreed set of measures/objectives can be a comfort to the individual undertaking the task in that they know exactly what is expected by when and can work to certain milestones getting several tiers of achievement from the whole process.

T – Tell others it is happening and attribute any glory to them

Telling others of the process has several important functions. First, it clarifies and announces the power set up so that the task is truly delegated over and staff work with and for the allocated individual with greater respect and enthusiasm. It is also important as undertaking the tasks will be even more motivated by the recognition they receive for a good job. Of course, it works the other way if things go a bit wrong. Rather than stand in the shadows to allow the limelight to shine on the individual where things are positive, the great leader will step up alongside the individual when things go wrong to ensure that they do not face the music alone.

When things go right, deferred glory is a stronger plus for the leader than trying to snatch it directly but it works the opposite way when things are negative. Sharing the mistakes and shouldering the responsibility alongside the subordinate ensures that they try again on another task and shows the bond that leader has with their staff.

E – Establish a positive delegating culture

Setting the example above will cultivate a culture of positive and developing delegation where staff trust you and are willing to try new things and expand their skills portfolio without resent. By ensuring they have a reputation for fairness, the great leader will not be judged on more petty things like "cherry picking" tasks but on the fact that everything has a useful and recognized purpose.

Such a culture of delegation glues together the team members more for the long term and also encourages staff retention because of a higher job satisfaction. It also ensures that the company is more flexible internally and externally, so sickness can easily be covered and competition more easily fought.

In addition to these positive effects on the company for the long term in achieving a truly engaged workforce, the example set will be replicated by those who lead further down the line. They will learn that the benefits of thought beforehand really do come out with a higher dividend in the end. In turn, they will practice the same positive delegation so training others in a self-sustaining and self-perpetuating way. These subcultures are important as the leader cannot be in every place and so needs that proxy presence throughout the hierarchy. This means that the leader will also have to invest time in training, supporting, and following through those who are that proxy so that the subdelegation is as effective as if they had administered the process themselves.

Communication channels

Communication channels are the final item on the checklist for achieving a high level of buy in and ultimate engagement. This is a huge area for discussion, as the channels are many and the cascades subject to many possible blocks and misunderstandings. From the sender to the recipient there are many potential areas for misunderstanding in terms of things such as the actual method of communication used to the securing feedback from that recipient. A whole chapter could be devoted to this subject but a more 360 degree look at the subject may better serve the executive purpose.

In terms of using the most effective levels of communication to achieve the "buy in" the communication process of sender to recipient needs to be linked or paralleled with the overall corporate direction in terms of the original vision, the broken down subvision parts within the company and the further broken down tasks which achieve these two.

Thus, it is more than mere delegation which will really firm up engagement. The great leader must bring together the skills used in surfacing sentiments, finding ways through, and add their knowledge of how long the communication cascade realistically takes to the convoluted nature of the systems design – however well intentioned it is. On top of this, they need to understand how to use their subleaders within that hierarchy and set up a spirit of empowerment and open communication. Sounds perfect! Needless to say that the real world does not offer this up without a good deal of hard work and the leader must start to cultivate a polylogue approach which promotes clarity if they are to achieve this level of engagement with their staff and their staff with the company and them.

Case study comment

Cultivating clarity

"The one I keep coming back to is clarity. Making it absolutely clear, the process I've gone through to get to the position I've taken and then the fact that I've thought through the knock on effects of that including no sweetening of the pill in terms of the effects on the people. I took 2 or 3 compliments in that period where I would go for example, I remember going to the headquarters of the estate agency business to tell them about the sale of the estate agency business and to whom it was sold which was a big, big issue for them, this was not a comfortable organisation we sold them to. I gave them a really quite difficult announcement and then got thanked afterwards for the empathy and the way I did that, because this was an organisation that I'd worked with for years. I understood them, I knew them, I liked them and rated them as a business, it's just that estate agency was not profitable enough to be part of a bank. So genuinely understanding what its like to be a line manager, or indeed a line supervisor when these sort of announcements land down from a high, I think was important for me. The fact that I've worked in the business understood the

▶

business, and stood shoulder by shoulder with them for a long time, was an important part of the way in which I approached it. I hadn't been parachuted in from another organisation, with all sorts of ingoing prejudices and just slash and burn with a clear conscience, so I think people genuinely understood the fact that some of what I was saying was uncomfortable for me, but had to be done and that's the way I would express it and explain exactly why."

Steven Crawshaw, CEO, Bradford and Bingley Plc

Walk the talk

Using the previously isolated PPODs and perception pathways, mark in the potential blocks in communication and marry each with a preventive action.

Polylogue

Polylogue is the multiple dialogue of simultaneous conversations which need to exist within a company for most effective use of the effort and experience within. It unlocks the existing potential from within toward the overall vision making the company more long-lived for it. The act of embracing the multidirectional dialogue of many and often conflicting opinion ensures the most informed environment possible but it takes a strong leader to allow the room for it to thrive.

By undertaking this approach, the leader knows that a team of individuals stand more chance of providing what the organization actually needs than they do alone and the competitive advantage increased by using the whole ability of that team to full effect. By ensuring, the energy of that whole team is channeled upwards toward the vision, with as few diversions and other agendas as possible, corporate performance is pushed faster toward its targets. All opinion, even that which is against some of the strategic decisions is heard and heard in fair forum. All views are incorporated into the way forward after appropriate and respectful debate and discussion. Therefore, polylogue is not just about good communication, it is about all communication and some of that communication may be uncomfortable. The true spirit of polylogue allows this discomfort the same space as the opinions which fit the current thinking.

The skill of perfecting polylogue lies in the ability to motivate and direct followers in a certain way, value the input they gain from those followers, and pull it upwards in one direction for the good of all. This is after it has been given the room and the time to thrive horizontally and in multidirections through the organization. This also involves working the views of their coleaders at different levels in the company into the overall corporate plan.

Previously, it has much been the case that coleaders have had to live in the shadow of the overall figurehead. Polylogue principles do not suggest the removal of that figurehead – more the use of their leadership in a different way. The polylogue leader brings out the coleaders from the shadows and uses their power and views to take the company forward in the same direction. The coleaders do not have to sacrifice their ideas to the figurehead – they get the glory for them at source. This way internal resent or conflict is reduced and they really are on the leader's side pushing the same vision – not their own agenda. Given the power and the glory, they are also more likely to pass on vital information and render the communication links more fluid, transparent, and effective as they are able to furnish their teams with a more relaxed respect for all the various views.

Therefore, leading followers toward a common goal and visioning pathways at many levels and through many others is key to performance success. More than that, valuing the talent and diversity of the multilevel coleaders within the organization will strengthen the organization to deal with fast-moving change.

This makes things sound easy but the mere handling of such a range of opinions and personalities requires a communication ability that can operate with an open approach collecting the varied input and also using it appropriately. As well as being approachable and ensuring a transparent communication system, leaders must be confident enough to be able to allow others to shine and not feel threatened by new talent and different opinion. This is an altruistic stance where they think less of themselves and more about the overall good of the company.

This communication is about connection as well as hierarchical cascade and promotes a shared responsibility for the overall vision as well as the individual delegated tasks. A community is literally created from this level of communication which is not just about sharing but about respect for others. The differing opinions within can be valued and compromises made. Vigorous exchange of ideas is encouraged with a solution target without denying anyone their voice. This gives overall decisions a true validity and with such an organic origin, it is much more likely to be wholeheartedly tried by those who have been involved in its inception.

Polylogue, with this level of interaction provides a platform for healthy debate and from that comes a more considered approach and real meaning at the operational levels that really matter. With such multilevel representation of the company, the resulting decisions are more likely to be the right ones as they were reached through collaborative dialogues which have sought lateral opinion rather than the two-dimensional ones achieved through a more traditional linear approach. Also because they are voluntary, staff really do participate because they want to rather than have to.

Instead of a simple authoritarian cascade of information from one representative leader at the top through a series of dutiful but sometimes reluctant followers who enact their instructions with varying degrees of exactness, this approach involves a three-dimensional, cooperative attitude and latitude of inclusivity. This feeds directly into the strategic plan which is better fed and more appropriate to its market, thanks to the "real" information it has received. Being able to hear things outside of that we want to is a key strength of the polylogue approach and followers feel better for having a real power to influence matters where their expertise is relevant. Sometimes that expertise can be more relevant than that of the leader so this trust is essential.

This *shared leadership* does actually empower leaders at different levels in the company. They not only have a voice but also have not been insulted by a token empowerment where they have little voice or power. They feel they truly own the situation with that direct influence on the decision-making process in the organization. The shared meanings and mutual respect become self-perpetuating and a positive culture of open and multiple dialogue starts to support itself. The happier the staff within this more honest and happier environment, they are more likely to stay longer and therefore become even more committed and useful in terms of their residual skills to the organization. New staff benefit from the start as they enter and learn this democracy and respect for others from scratch. Information and responsibility are shared and a polylogue platform is built where all learn, trust, and work together.

Case study comment

Cultivating clarity

"Battles are won and lost by communication and it is how you can communicate, whether you can communicate, the way in which you communicate that matters. You can say the same sentence and it will mean different things by the way you say it, by the emphasis you put on different words. If I was to say to you 'I was born in London', I could say that five different ways and it would mean five different things. Once the addresser has said the words, they belong to the addressee and they interpret them as they want from their own agenda, from what has happened in their past life, but that will be their perspective. So it is very, very important to get communication right and to get the right

▶

attitude and to get the right interpretation. Also to ask questions, so often we don't ask the right questions and sometimes we assume a situation and assume that the other person has understood what we are saying. I had a situation on the telephone the other day, when I was given some information and I assumed that they understood everything that I was saying, but in fact I did not ask the right questions and consequently it did not work out. Now knowing that even though I think the other person has understood what I am saying, I am going to ask them my questions, because everybody is different and everybody looks at a situation from their own agenda rather than looking at it objectively."

Rona Cant – Adventurer

This all sounds great and indeed it is but what is the down side of such democracy and collegiality? Well, it takes longer and involves more patience. So, the great leader must factor this in.

The leader must allow time for information and opinions to be reflected on properly and debated to satisfaction before decisions are reached and moved forward. With more opinion allowed in so many different directions, delays are likely so the leader must be able to furnish the environment for this as well as be politically sensitive and approachable.

There is a danger with such a lot of information and opinion opened up within the company that it can travel in many directions if not controlled. Indeed, this would be an even greater problem than not having the information at all. The leader, therefore, must control the situation and ensure that the wealth of information is used wisely and that argument is kept at a healthy level – which requires a good deal of skill.

It is also necessary to evaluate all the management systems which would hold this in place. Meetings, company newsletters, e-mail cultures, and so on all provide the mechanics for the information to flow through. As well as being a conduit, the system also has to capture information readily. Such choices and use of media are key to the success of the spiritual intent and the leader may have to make certain compromises too. All too often, the difference between the ideal and what is actually achievable is greater than we would like.

Although the polylogue approach takes more time it is more holistic and in the longer term hardier.

Patience is rewarded with the polylogue practice. If coleaders or subleaders can thrive without feeling threatened and can work with a sense of ownership and satisfaction, then they will pass this onto their staff and allow them the same room too. There is no doubt it does take a lot of confidence to take on this approach but once done it is replicated throughout the business and brings back reward many times over.

Great rate

This chapter has touched on some of the elements of "engaging." It is not a definitive list but the elements which seem to make the difference involve

Buy In

Communication Channels

Cultivating Clarity

Delegation

Emotional Commitment

Empowerment

Polylogue

Shared Leadership

Willing Effort

CHAPTER 6

Driving for success

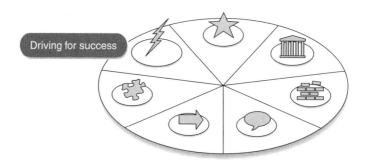

Source: Compiled by authors

Chapter introduction

Performance and purpose push-pull
Setting and monitoring performance targets and measures which align with the overall strategic aims and ensure security for all

Hard line audit with soft line plaudit
Balancing inspection with affection and projection to achieve results

Staying power
Formulating longetivity life lines and recession proofing to increase leader and follower shelf life

Burn out
Diagnosing, anticipating, and preventing the condition

Now that visions have been created and with considerable effort, thought and foresight, the leader has achieved a high level of buy in and communication from all levels of their following to arrive at a successful starting point, they must continue the drive for success by setting firm controls to stay there.

Staying power as well as stamina comes into the equation to seal the hard work so far, channel it in the right direction, but more importantly ensure that good and best practice as well as hard earned progress stays there and moves forward for the benefit of the company and of course the keen contributors.

Staying power is not just about the skin thickness and shelf life of the leader themselves in this instance. Staying power is also about audit and performance systems and procedures which embrace the energy, analyze it, and repeat it where it is good and refine it where it is not.

Driving for successful performance can often be as much of a "push" as a "pull". Success must be driven and achieved with a complete buy in from the followers, stretching them just enough but not too much.

Performance targets will have been set from the original vision and strategic plan and now broken down into the necessary component parts. The calculation and measurement of these is a necessary and important part of ensuring success though perhaps regarded as one of the less glamorous sides of the leadership portfolio of responsibility. This is not just about making the scientific audit of progress a standard and respected part of events but making it a framework of security for all, the company, the leader and the actual followers involved in providing the energy, drive and data.

Walk the talk

Randomly retrieve five different levels of performance targets from different areas in your organization. Evaluate how they feed into the strategic direction.

Driving for success is in part the drive of the leader but it is also the encapsulation of the willing drive of the follower in a controlled environment where everyone knows exactly what they need to do and by when.

Internal controls need to be in place with agreed targets so regular checks on actual performance against those desired or predicted are made. Even more importantly, these need to be assessed at every level to ensure they are not only meeting the strategic need but also fulfilling and developing the individuals and teams producing the results. The participation of working to performance criteria should be pleasurable in the main and leave the participant with a sense of satisfaction overall. When things go wrong, as inevitably they will occasionally, this is used as a positive experience and constructively improved upon to realign with target.

Performance measurement, management, and motivation are not short term although short-term targets are part of the overall picture. A three dimensional perspective of how all activities contribute to long-term events and long-term targets is essential and benchmarking and variance analysis are used in a positive feedback culture. Staying power is only possible if the short-term activities really do line up with the long-term aims and the personal needs of the followers are managed as efficiently and as importantly as the audit systems. It is important that the softer people skills from the leader are implemented at the same time as this scientifically driven pushing. Each of these motivators are essential and equal components of target achievement and as important as the measurement itself.

The great leader will enforce the audit systems with grace and sensitivity but with firmness and fairness. Getting the followers to "churn out" the output involves assessing ability too so that they consider their "learn out" point ensuring the follower is not under or over used. This must be carefully judged so they all are pushed to the best of that ability but not in danger of "burn out." The systems therefore must be bought in by all too so they provide as much protection as they do projection and inspection.

Performance and purpose push-pull

Aside from the skill of visioning to inspire staff and pull then toward the overall goals, the great leader needs to scientifically break down separate activities at each process level in the company to make sure they align with the joint direction along with the psychological "buy in" levels of the staff. Science and art move hand in hand to push the operation forward.

A breakdown of key performance indicators need to be established from the larger goal and agreed with the participants. These segmentalized activities will in themselves create purpose and pull as well as link to that of the company. An understanding of the "rubric" of activities is essential so that norms are established right at the heart of the operational machine and these norms are accurately calculated to ensure that their accumulation adds up to the whole need or even better beyond it. Allowances need to be made for delays, sickness, holidays, so a standard activity card must have a bit of a buffer in its make up. Such activity card standards can work well for all. The leader can assess day-to-day performance against such a bench mark to isolate development needs quickly and effectively and avoid any nasty shortfall surprises in the bigger picture when all is through wash up stage. By having the exact activity expectations clear at the most basic level small security frameworks are created for those expected to do them as well as those who expect them done. These activity rubrics are key to maximizing use of time and lining it up with the larger targets.

The basic management information can provide a number of starting points depending on the nature of the business. Average invoice values, footfall conversions, are useful indicators for discussion at all levels. Increasing their meaning and importance by overlaying the average activity which produces them makes their meaning all the more pertinent and clear to all. If, for example, a member of staff knows that a certain average number of client visits achieves a certain average amount of income and this is part of the fabric of their day-to-day work, not just a monthly comment from the profit and loss sheet, they are more likely to be pulled toward doing that extra bit of work before they go and push themselves to achieve that reachable but small target.

Where such practice is not the norm at this basic level, that small push is not made from within and the repercussional effect of this on the individual and the company is much greater than is instantly apparent. The loss of one small client visit because of that momentary lack of push or pull seems insignificant in itself but when multiplied by the whole staff numbers and the formed norm in practice of each of those individuals, the calculation of lost opportunity and lost income is more than a little surprising when looked at from an accumulated perspective.

So, each activity has its direct value on the corporate purse or service standards and this focus needs to become a language or currency at the relevant level. Talking in terms of such exact conversion at the front line is as important as calculating it retrospectively in the back office. It is at source that split second decisions are made which push or pull the activity toward the overall figure. If the cultural norm is a *line leader* pointing out in a friendly way – "Hey – do you know if you manage just one more of those before tomorrow, the team will have reached half way". This friendly and encouraging push of the staff member toward the pull of the target embeds a safety net for all. The encouragement is more likely to bring results than a retrospective punitive session deflating the staff member regarding their shortfalls.

This is less about leaders negatively focusing on what isn't done directly to staff and more on what could be done in a positive and even better, willing, way. Of course, *line leaders* need to isolate missed opportunities or deficits in performance and ensure they are addressed but thinking carefully about the approach may double the difference in output.

Goal setting

Key performance indicators such as revenue and quality are the litmus tests which indicate levels of success. These indicators are used as pivots for specific targets – usually monetary or standards – and from here the specific activities can be related to their achievement. The specific activities are the *kinetic performance indicators* in which they actually deliver the correct energy and motion toward the key performance indicators. Kinetic Performance Indicators are those of the finest detail – the "doing detail" which drives the way forward. They feed into the key performance indicators which are the quantifiable quotients which snapshot progress toward the overall goal. Such definition and measurement is in itself key to management analysis which is driven forward rather than merely a look at past events which financial information used in isolation tends to encourage. Kinetic Performance Indicators (KPI 2s) are level two indicators – borne of the initial driving pivots Key performance Indicators (KPI 1s). They can then be further broken down into a front line or exact activity or Key Performance Driver (KPA).

Key performance activities (KPAs) are actions such as visits, phone calls, service checks, quality checks – ie, the every day tasks at the front line. The difference is the drive. Great leaders will turn these tasks toward the overall direction and ensure they are also measured. Less great leaders will leave them to look after themselves. The former approach makes certain that nothing is left to chance and efforts are not wasted doing the wrong things. Staff can be well intentioned with efforts but put themselves and the company in danger by being misguided by incorrect leadership approval or encouragement. For example, huge efforts into mailshots or producing fancy leaflets is admirable but useless if not channeled into a rubric of critical success activities which feed into the overall critical success factors of the organization. Staff can appear very busy doing all the wrong things and then be down hearted when the KPIs show up a poor performance because basically this energy has just filtered down into a large black hole and not produced results. Results are all and are not achieved by accident. A real concerted effort by the leader and then the staff is needed to ensure the correct foci are attended to in order to bring about that required result. Indeed failing businesses or departments, and the business doctors among you will recognize the symptoms, are often spotted by the defensive behavior of the teams for their input. Successful units tend to have a flexible approach toward constructive improvements, less successful ones will invest their time protecting their original and own cause. Always a good sign of the business temperature either way! It is a leadership failing to allow staff to do this and for the inevitable internal politics to further pollute the business environment. The great leader will see through the defense of how much effort went into what and constructively analyze the actual output from the highly acclaimed input.

So, we touch on efficiency and effectiveness, almost by accident. The KPIs and the details of the KPAs are mentioned in the interests of effectiveness. Effectiveness being acknowledged as a quality of achievement toward the progress in the direction chosen rather than that of efficiency where a quantity drive is the main drive for the leader. Although, it should be said that quantification is important in the measurement of progress, and indeed, it is the definition of and the measurement of certain indicators which actually barometer the performance of an organization. Perhaps what we are saying here is that this performance is also about that of the individuals and what they contribute to the overall which counts toward the big picture, not just in quantity terms but in quality ones.

Performance management tools have evolved to take this into account and models such as the Balanced Score Card have been in operation for some time. These take four indicators usually in the areas of customer feeling, internal systems, financial detail and organizational learning and development and use them to measure progress in a forward thinking way. Performance against such indicators allows for a gap analysis to be made and improvement to be decided to keep to the original strategic plan.

Such tools are very useful but only if used throughout the levels in the organization and only if translated to the KPA front line level. Monthly reporting mechanisms at KPI level need to inform the decision makers in the right way – ie forward and with the right level of detail. It is part of the leadership role to predict the different necessary detail which will feed into the overall mechanism and then also to translate them into KPA form. This way each activity has a role and adds a transparent value to the overall indicator. So if it is the number of students on a training course that is the critical success factor or measure at a training centre, the client visits to the appropriate client or telephone calls to them will be the KPA which need monitoring or measuring to ensure the correct numbers are attracted to and on the courses. This will be in addition to the regular service calls from that centre as well as the quality of provision to ensure further recommendations and future as well as retained business. It sounds simple and often it is. A failing training unit can easily be spotted by the lack of these KPAs at front line as well as the obvious lack of specific commercial income. The KPIs in this instance will be the service quality in terms of overall evaluation, the actual throughput of student numbers, the profit in commercial terms and so the story continues.

Walk the talk

Chart your business KPIs and now make them kinetic. Translate each one into several KPAs on a monthly basis.

The effective leader will not just be able to spot the lack of activity at one end and the lack of profit the other, but implement the appropriate science and suggest the appropriate training to remedy the mess. Positional power is useful in this instance, as is support from higher levels, as it is not unusual for failing individuals or teams to make a lot of noise to divert attention away from the problem – enter coffee cup cartels and inward looking political partisans. Those frightened of having their failure highlighted may act dramatically, those open to constructive feedback will listen with grace.

Hard line audit with soft line plaudit

Balancing inspection with affection and projection to achieve results is both a science and an art. Worried staff are not only less productive but also sometimes destructive. It follows – if a failing individual gets worried and is perhaps too proud to accept development, then making the organization or other individuals look bad can alleviate some of their pain in the short term and divert attention from themselves. These diversions are expensive and the great leader can avoid them by bedding in routine inspection tools which are not only easy to use but also help the initially worried individual feel more secure themselves. Hard line audit of activity inspection need not be an unpleasant obligation of ticking off tasks. Staff can be encouraged to collate their own statistics and assess them against previously set norms.

The leader will have calculated the necessary activities up front allowing room for some changes of course and then perhaps formulated a method of record/tabulation for the figures to be collated and made transparent with ease. Setting in the norms and reinforcing their necessity and role sets in expectations from the word go. This provides more reassurance when done with inclusion and discussion rather than a pencil sharpening officiousness. Everyone knows what is "expected" and the data is jointly owned so more enthusiasm goes into its completion. Everyone also knows what is going to be "inspected" or variance so extra attempts will be made to satisfy previously agreed targets.

The hard line of audit need not be unpleasant. It gives a safe base for all on which to judge and comment and such data mechanisms are usually only a problem for those who frankly are failing and do not want that made transparent. Those who are doing what is required of them and perhaps more will be pleased to see the efforts recorded and used constructively. It is a leadership skill to implement these audit tools with the right spirit and encourage their correct and positive use. *Activity Based Calculators* – see Tables 6.1, 6.2, and 6.3 – provide an easy framework within which to work and from which to discuss ground level business. Once this is done, they almost become self developing and self perpetuating. A culture of, as well as a structure of, accountability is woven into the fabric of the organization and staff are encouraged to use performance as an enhancement tool rather than one associated with punishment.

Table 6.1 Activity based calculator – monthly

KPI	KPI	KPI	Monthly income calculator		KPA 2	KPA 3	KPA 4
			KPA 1				
Target income	ATV	No. of transactions	No. of ints per month	No. of ints per week	CVs	Jobs & regs	BD calls
40000	2500	16	80	20	560	64	640
25000	2000	12.5	63	16	438	50	500
24000	2000	12	60	15	420	48	480
23000	2000	11.5	58	14	403	46	460
22000	2000	11	55	14	385	44	440
21000	2000	10.5	53	13	368	42	420
20000	2000	10	50	13	350	40	400
19000	2000	9.5	48	12	333	38	380
18000	2000	9	45	11	315	36	360
17000	2000	8.5	43	11	298	34	340
16000	2000	8	40	10	280	32	320
15000	2000	7.5	38	9	263	30	300
14000	2000	7	35	9	245	28	280
13000	2000	6.5	33	8	228	26	260
12000	2000	6	30	8	210	24	240
11000	2000	5.5	28	7	193	22	220
10000	2000	5	25	6	175	20	200
9000	2000	4.5	23	6	158	18	180

Table 6.2 Activity based calculator – weekly

KPI	KPI	KPI	KPA 1	Weekly	KPA 2	KPA 3	KPA 4	KPA 2	KPA 3	KPA 4
Target income	ATV	No. of transactions	No. of ints per month	No. of ints per week	CVs	Jobs & regs	BD calls	CVs	Jobs & regs	BD calls
20000	2500	8	40	10	280	32	320	70	8	80
19000	2000	9.5	48	12	333	38	380	83	10	95
18000	2000	9	45	11	315	36	360	79	9	90
17000	2000	8.5	43	11	298	34	340	74	9	85
16000	2000	8	40	10	280	32	320	70	8	80
15000	2000	7.5	38	9	263	30	300	66	8	75
14000	2000	7	35	9	245	28	280	61	7	70
13000	2000	6.5	33	8	228	26	260	57	7	65
11000	2000	5.5	28	7	193	22	220	48	6	55
10000	2000	5	25	6	175	20	200	44	5	50
9000	2000	4.5	23	6	158	18	180	39	5	45
8000	2000	4	20	5	140	16	160	35	4	40
7000	2000	3.5	18	4	123	14	140	31	4	35
6000	2000	3	15	4	105	12	120	26	3	30
5000	2000	2.5	13	3	88	10	100	22	3	25
4000	2000	2	10	3	70	8	80	18	2	20
3000	2000	1.5	8	2	53	6	60	13	2	15
2000	2000	1	5	1	35	4	40	9	1	10

NB: Shaded areas are weekly data borne of monthly data on white

Table 6.3 Activity based calculator – daily

KPA 1		Monthly			Weekly			Daily		
		KPA 2	KPA 3	KPA 4	KPA 2	KPA 3	KPA 4	KPA 2	KPA 3	KPA 4
No. ints per month	No. ints per week	CVs	Jobs & regs	BD calls	CVs	Jobs & regs	BD calls	CVs	Jobs & regs	BD calls
40	10	280	32	320	70	8	80	14	2	16
48	12	333	38	380	83	10	95	17	2	19
45	11	315	36	360	79	9	90	16	2	18
43	11	298	34	340	74	9	85	15	2	17
40	10	280	32	320	70	8	80	14	2	16
38	9	263	30	300	66	8	75	13	2	15
35	9	245	28	280	61	7	70	12	1	14
33	8	228	26	260	57	7	65	11	1	13
28	7	193	22	220	48	6	55	10	1	11
25	6	175	20	200	44	5	50	9	1	10
23	6	158	18	180	39	5	45	8	1	9
20	5	140	16	160	35	4	40	7	1	8
18	4	123	14	140	31	4	35	6	1	7
15	4	105	12	120	26	3	30	5	1	6
13	3	88	10	100	22	3	25	4	1	5
10	3	70	8	80	18	2	20	4	0	4
8	2	53	6	60	13	2	15	3	0	3
5	1	35	4	40	9	1	10	2	0	2

Case study comment

Brief in positively to gain acceptance

"When I was young I taught that others have to do what you tell them to do, you can say I was a bit dictatorial. Then I went to the US to study at the Harvard Business School and I found to my surprise that things don't work like that, there is a need for discussion and listening to what others have to say. That your ideas need to be accepted by others, this is especially important in politics."

Olivier Giscard d'Estaing

Former member of the French Parliament

Chairman of the European League for Economic cooperation and the Committee for a World Parliament (COPAM)

Founder and Chairman, INSEAD (European Institute of Business Administration)

Once in place the value of the data is more than just the moment it is in. The aged data regarding input can be accumulated and correlations made with output, trends isolated and decisions made early in the process or system to change direction in order to stick to the overall goal. This data analysis can be in the form of positive discussion about gaps and about successes with positive and quick actions which remedy any digression from the main target. Such data analysis can also be used to pinpoint staff development needs quickly and encourage staff retention as weaknesses can simply become areas for further development and tackled quickly and positively in the early stages of the loop. This further reassures the employee and in the long term widens their own portfolio of skills which can then be used on the organization. For example, if a business development executive was failing to meet targets to get delegates on a particular training course it would be really easy to spot where to help them remedy the situation from the activity data they supply. This could be a constructive discussion isolating the particular activity which needs attention followed by the training they need. If they were calling and mailshotting to the point of fatigue but still not getting the delegates to come forward, the answer obviously lies in their technique. This can be remedied, quickly and easily and save a lot of company time in potential time off sick because of their stress or potential politics to draw attention away from the problem. So, it is not just about being efficient, it is also an approach to unsurface effectiveness. If many calls are being made and much effort put in then it is a crying shame to see it wasted when more effective use of that effort can be easily directed.

The great leader will apply this and support the use of constructive frameworks to make activity and data transparent, the not so great leader will either accept the excuses and diversions of failure, allow poor performance and politics to rule or be punitive in approach and cause much the same damage.

There is of course always the possibility that one also encounters laziness on the way too, this can be dealt with in a constructive way by gentle peer comparison and guidance as to the correct amounts of activity to achieve the goal.

Hard line audit methods are a sound investment for any organization. This is front line hard line audit – not strategic use of monthly management information. Daily activities in detail all make up that whole and need to be treated in the same way and with the same respect as monthly management information. A variance analysis of actual against set activities is as important so front line duties are flexed in the same way as the larger key performance indicator budgets and actuals regularly are. Such flexing becomes the norm and gears the organization up for more readiness for change from the inside.

As well as trends in KPAs over time to assess effectiveness as well as efficiency, the same data tools can be used for planning around future events such as holidays. The KPAs can be calculated to allow for annual leave allowances, seasonal peaks/troughs in business and service, and using a safely calculated scientific formula provide educated guestimates of whether targets will be achievable well ahead of the game. These baselines can filter into more strategic planning such as the recruitment of more staff to make the grade as well as be used as a guideline for the need for incentives to ensure that extra push.

These KPAs soon become common ground level currency and filter into the day-to-day time management of the individuals. They begin to translate their work into more specific outputs naturally and begin a more unconscious approach as well as a conscious one.

This natural and more organic move to incorporate the science into the work softens the hard line of outright audit. Further softening then occurs in the form of recognition and praise for the good work done. Soft line plaudit means a show of real appreciation for the effort put in and ensuring the right level of recognition is given to the individual for making that effort. They can see just where their effort has fitted into the bigger pictures at different levels, giving it real meaning and purpose. So control and inspection need not be unpleasant. It can actually, if implemented with the right spirit, create a positive vehicle for good work to be clearly shown and appreciated.

If this positivity extends to clear record keeping then a further level of management information is available to the leader to help make more appropriate decisions at the heart of the business.

Example

To demonstrate the translation of KPIs to KPAs for daily use a set of three tables will give a simple illustration of how staff could be presented with a more exact framework to their tasks. (Tables 6.1, 6.2, and 6.3)

The example is taken from a fee income area but could equally be adapted to activities toward a service or quality. In the example a target income is set and the leader will also set out a rubric of norms which would, on average, be held to achieve those income figures. The cells are set up to enable the leader to punch in the target they require and the formulae within the cells does the rest. In this case the income is fees from recruitment placement and the activities chosen are those day-to-day tasks such as business development calls, no. of CVs sent to employers, no. of candidates and jobs registered, no. of interviews, and so on. which bring about those fees.

The leader will set the norm framework and in this case it is

- five interviews to make one average transaction
- seven CVs out to create one interview
- one average transaction per four jobs or four candidates registered
- Ten business development calls per job created

Naturally this is adaptable to the KPAs the leader thinks appropriate to the income generation. Other KPAs could be added – for instance no. of client visits. For the purpose of this example though the above KPAs have been chosen to illustrate the ease of translation to weekly and daily levels of activity. Simple formulas on the spreadsheet allow for easy translation and staff can be included to devise these tools in minutes.

Walk the talk

Chart your monthly KPAs using a simple spreadsheet as shown. Now translate them into weekly and daily activities as shown. Set up some blank spreadsheets and sell in the benefits of their use to one or some of your teams as a pilot.

Factors affecting performance

Naturally, the science and good intentions are all very well but they cannot be considered without a proper regard for the "human" producing the tasks/data which make them up – the *art* of management and leadership. As well as concentrating on implementing a positive system of transparency as far as KPAs are concerned the performance enhancement of the individual must be considered carefully. Completing tasks to an instruction does not achieve that extra effort or understanding of the overall picture. The data simply becomes a restrictive framework if that is the case. The framework and rubrics only work if the employees set about the duties willingly and with the right understanding of their importance – theirs, that is, as well as the data.

Performance assessment should not be merely a check of actuals versus budget to discuss the variance of anything. That is merely a secretarial/administrative check and frankly leadership skills are not really needed for that bit. Performance appraisal should be holistic and respect the past, current, and future situation of the employee as well as achieving their willing effort through development and inspiration.

The great leader and then their representative leaders at all the other levels should assess a number of factors which affect the performance of the human being who works for them. They are not a machine and some may fall into the trap of getting lost behind the science of achieving targets/budgets. It is important to remember that these scientific tools are just that – a means of helping the overall direction – they are not the direction themselves. They are partial drivers toward success, not the whole picture.

Performance appraisals vary in different companies and in many the appraisal has lost its value. Some purely target-driven individuals assess their staff to one rubric only and then find that there is little respect for the appraisal process in its lack of development focus or human regard. If data or scientific rubrics are used in this way then staff become skeptical of their use as they do the appraisal. The collated data with trends and so on should be used to constructively isolate areas for driver change in the focus of certain KPAs feeding into certain KPIs. This discussion should be geared toward selecting development opportunities for the staff to improve themselves in a more rounded way and feel more secure and confident in achieving the targets set. Further though opportunities for motivation and observing the situational factors in which the employee works are also important.

During appraisal and ongoing reviews of performance the ART of qualitative data is as important as the quantitative data just discussed. To gain such feedback and be informed by softer means each performance assessment should contain an ART approach. ART is

ABILITY

RESTRICTIONS

TRAINING & DEVELOPMENT

Ability

Through performance management processes such as appraisal interview the leader must make a fair assessment of the ability of the employee. This should be carefully done and not haloed or horned by one piece of behavior, success, or failure. Many a narrow-minded manager has pigeon holed a potentially good employee because they have had one bad attempt at something or they make the presumption that they cannot do something. Also it is not just about the current ability of the member of staff but also the potential they have. The ability of the employee should not only be judged by the appraising superior but also any immediate supervisor and, where it is appropriate, fellow workers.

Appraisal processes in organizations should be developmental rather than mere statistical reviews of performance. In fact really the two should be kept apart. The Performance Reviews should be regularly part of the communication process and be two way – that is, the employee reviewing themselves and reporting it upwards as well as being reviewed downwards by their superior. An appraisal should then cater for the human and developmental needs of the individual, pinpointing particular training to help them improve or further their career. It should be a positive and motivating process, which as well as tackling any awkward issues, leaves the individual with a corporate spirit and a clear road on which to set their willing efforts.

All too often the yearly or half-yearly appraisal interview becomes an administrative formality which ticks boxes rather than truly inspires and pushes an individual further on. With many an ill-prepared manager/leader grabbing the previous form from the previous year just before the coming appraisal session and then whizzing through it as if it is something to be gotten through rather than enjoyed and utilized to the full, it is no wonder then that many an employee treats the process with considerable disdain, skepticism, and low value.

Restrictions

There will be a number of internal and external influences or restrictions on the performance of any individual. It should be remembered that when expecting certain tasks and outputs from this person, one should realize that they also have a life outside of work and that can affect their performance considerably.Family events and pressures are likely, so should not be a surprise and it is important to accommodate some flexibility to help where needed. Usually this is greatly appreciated and the company will be rewarded many times over by the employee who having been treated in such a considerate way willingly gives more on return. Of course, the targets must still be met and some inclusion of any deficit must be made into other targets to make up the ground. In addition to this external environmental influence, there are of course other external influences to consider such as economical factors which may have an effect on what is actually achievable and what is not. Seasonal peaks, exchange rates, base products costs, and so on can all be factors which filter through the KPIs to the KPAs.

Internally, restrictions may exist in the working environment. From the physical space in which the employee works to the relationships that they have with colleagues and superiors. Even down to the confidence the employees have in themselves. The personal relationship staff have with their direct superior is worth a closer look from time to time. Personality and political differences can make a big difference to performance. Where an employee feels well represented and supported and motivated to the right degree, performance will more than likely have more stamina to last a longer course. Where these start to fall down because of bad relationships resulting in less than accurate representation from the superior and more coercion than incentive, a short and temporary performance blast may be achieved. This, however, is borne of fear but nothing more follows it and certainly no willing effort is channeled into the performance process from the individual subjected to the coercion and who by now does not trust the manager. It also then follows that free communication is impeded by this reluctance and this further affects the competitive workings of the whole company never mind the individual.

Equally, an observation of roles/tasks and even job descriptions can be useful to the leader who wants more than mere efficiency. It can be interesting how very finite job descriptions can impede a flexible liaison between colleagues and ultimately restrict fluidity and willingness. Clarity of role and purpose is important but not taken to the extent of divisional autocratism.

Training and development

Each employee should be afforded a training needs analysis in their own right as well as departmental and corporate level ones and proper personal development plans made from appraisals and performance reviews. The differentiation between training and development is also important. Of course it is important to ensure that employees provide the skills necessary toward the overall goal in terms of training which is always in the corporate interest. It is also imperative to provide personal development for the individual so each is self-actualized. This benefits the employee directly but naturally has positive knock on effects for the company if those same individuals are able to give more in wider and wider terms.

It would be wise then to ascertain a mix of training and development which benefits all parties and provides the best levels of flexibility as well as motivation and job and self-enrichment. If this could all be achieved in line with the strategic plan and vision then all the better.

Such training and development approaches will not only increase the portfolio of skills from which the company and the employee will benefit but also as a positive by-product increase the self-esteem of the employee. This self-esteem will be that they have internally about how they see themselves, that they have in terms of how they think others see them and that they have about themselves in particular situations. This investment will bring reward and most likely increase the staying time and power of the employee which in turn increases the staying power of the company.

Walk the talk

Apply ART to three of your employees of different levels and then have your direct reporting leaders do the same. Discuss your findings at your next management meeting and derive some actions from the process.

Staying power

Formulating longetivity life lines at all levels of the organization is important. Staying power is more than that of the visible leader, although that is a key issue. Staying power is a power throughout the layers of the organization in terms of its systems and processes as well as its people. Recession proofing to increase leader and follower shelf life is as much a part of driving for success as individual activity direction and follower spirit is.

Driving for real success means longer term and more stable success rather than one-off successes here and there.

It would follow that some time would be needed to see manifested what one has initiated. It is not good for any organization to have too many changeovers and habitually short tenures for higher level positions. Corporate focus would then give way to individual survival of the recruited leader creating a conflict of interests. Equally a certain amount of time is needed so the leader can invest in many of the approaches discussed throughout this text. Getting to know the staff and their motivations toward gaining their willing efforts and opinions will require the security of a certain length of tenure. Without this security, the leader's focus cannot possibly be devoted to the organization. Equally, there are issues about outstaying one's welcome and a perception of this is wise.

Case study comment

Know the shelf life

"In politics, 2 terms of 5 years is sufficient, you need 2 terms to achieve your vision and things you said you were going to do. If you stay longer you have overstayed and you become stale. When I initiated INSEAD, I also stayed two terms as a Dean then I let others because you become stale, you have the same ideas and you start repeating the same speeches. Then it is time to move. In business you may need to stay longer, perhaps three terms, if it is not family business. Now even family businesses are going for professional managers so there is some movement."

Olivier Giscard d'Estaing

Former member of the French Parliament

Chairman of the European League for Economic cooperation and the Committee for a World Parliament (COPAM)

Founder and Chairman, INSEAD (European Institute of Business Administration)

Even with personal staying power and the security of tenure there will be dilemmas in driving for success. The decision making will be influenced by relationships and personalities to a certain extent as trust and bonds are formed so the complete impartiality of a purely scientific approach becomes less easy and some compromises are made between the scientific evidence and the repercussional effect on the human beings within.

This does uncover the possibility that targets could be set around relationships rather than corporate need so the great leader needs to ensure they compromise for the right reasons.

Compromises have to be made throughout the hierarchy

Case study comment

Compromises

"You learn how to relate to other people, how to listen to them, discover what their needs are and in turn you learn that you too can be loved despite all your mistakes, despite all your weak points and areas where you need to grow. I think this dynamic is very much a part of community life. When it comes to the point where you are discussing something as a full member, that is, somebody who is life committed through profession of final vows, you realize that there is a bond of love among you through that commitment. There are some things that you're not going to understand, some things that you're not going to agree with or some things that people are not going to agree with you about, but through that commitment and love, you can accept that in each other. I like to compare it to the ocean: on top of the ocean there can be storms, the waves can seem wild and it is work sometimes to just move against the winds. But deep down inside there's stillness, a depth, a peace that really sustains the ocean, sustains its life. I think it's the same with us, deep inside ourselves we know even if we don't always see eye to eye or we're upset about something or having a bad day or whatever, deep down inside the bond exists, the commitment is forever and you can ride the waves because of that deep inner source."

Sr. Judith Zoebelein, F.S.E., is a Franciscan Sister of the Eucharist, and founder of the Holy See's World Wide Web site on the Internet (www.vatican.va)

The great leader is also only as good as the staying power of their team and the right level of control and consideration has been discussed to further increase that and their subsequent productivity. It follows then that these become KPAs on the great leader's data collection sheet and that a KPI of note is attrition rate.

Burn out

Much of this text is devoted to increasing the staying power and shelf life of leaders by increasing their portfolio of skills to enable them to change when circumstances arise. By making themselves more adaptable to the situational changes and more observant of context and characters they are more likely to stand the test of time and accordingly increase their shelf life as well as that of their team. However, there is the flip side of the coin in that in driving for success a point of strain could be reached for that leader and also of course for their team. Diagnosing, anticipating, and preventing the condition of burn out must also be discussed as part of that drive forward.

As pressure increases in the workplace so does the likelihood that overload/strain points will be reached. These will vary from individual to individual and the great leader needs to have an idea of where their pressure point may be in different situations and then naturally also be aware of where that of others in their team may be.

Burn out may start out with subtle changes in behavior or may be quite sudden. Some leaders may suffer a "smiling depression" where no one knows their personal turmoil and then a sudden deterioration occurs. Others may let things slowly slip until a point of reluctant admission is reached. This then could be repeated throughout the hierarchy at all levels as each faces their own *limitation low*. Burn out and then the subsequent stress can be caused by a number of things in a pressurized environment. For example:

- Being penned in may be a familiar one for a candidate of a certain age. If domestic responsibilities require a certain level of material existence it may make it difficult to take the risks in a career to move on so allowing promotion to pass by.

- Ground hog day may be another situation where the repetition of certain tasks just tips someone over the edge because of the sheer relentless nature of events.
- "Streamlining soak up" may hit where companies have de-layered or re-layered and certain responsibilities now need to be soaked up by those already under pressure from the original portfolio of tasks.

Hitting these limitation lows is an inevitable part of pressurized working life so the leader should not be surprised when they appear either in their staff team or indeed, in themselves. In fact the more "normal" the leader treats the encounter then the more likely each candidate is likely to cope better. It may be that hitting limitation lows is a working necessity, a point that has to be reached by all so that real self-knowledge is achieved and a point from where each then picks themselves up. It may be that the coping of the situation actually strengthens the employee and makes them even better for the company.

Of course, burn out can be used as a bit of a weapon by the more manipulative manager. Many an employee will be scared of admitting what they see as weakness and some managers have been known to use this to their advantage. A "burn out bully" uses the limitation low point of an employee as a coercive power measure or punitive power as previously discussed. It is not that they push the employee toward the point until they crack at all – no – it is far more devious than that. They know the employee will not want to *admit the hit* so will use the possibility of its occurrence as a currency. Such managers can even represent their staff to their own superiors as more "stressed" or "burned out" than they actually are if they want to limit their progress or even make themselves look better. Talent envy from a threatened manager can drive the burn out symptoms underground and this may cause more damage. The great leader needs to worry more about the silent and the unsaid. Any outright conflict is annoying but healthy as it is the employee who is coping well. Those who cope less well are those who become more recessive and invisible with the symptoms.

The great leader also have their eye on how such burn out issues affect different layers and different types in their teams. For instance, gender pressures in terms of performance are often a common thread in the workforce. Where women are juggling domestic responsibilities with their work, it is less likely that they will *admit the hit* of burn out as they are carving out their equality. This can particularly slide across cultures. For instance, the Asian festival of Divali in November has its extra domestic pressures and responsibilities for the female but the workplace does not always recognize it is as important as Christmas in the Christian community. Potential hiding of burn out can also be seen in other ways to the internal competition of gender issues – age competition may be an issue in the workplace or talent competition.

With the acceptance that burn out and stress are components of the drive toward success, the great leader would be best prepared by having a *positive psychological policy* to embrace it and *EASE* it.

EASE
Empathy and Evaluation
Approachability, Access, and Achievement
Structure, Security, and Safety
Education

Empathy and evaluation

Take the time to talk about and tackle the issues and really understand them. This sounds very obvious but many ignore the symptoms thinking that they will just go away. This goes for the employee too. An empathic approach will help them recognize the situation and understand it which will speed up the process of development from it.

Approachability, access, and achievement

Assessing how our own leadership can be accessed is often very revealing. Where leaders think staff will talk to them readily it can often be found to be the opposite case. The leader can also help the employee break down and tackle certain of the issues by making them more accessible and help them approach each matter in manageable pieces. So a certain sense of achievement is gained by the employee which boosts their confidence and gives them further strength to tackle the next thing.

Structure, security, and safety

Providing a structure of attack on issues will help carve a way forward for the employee and the leader can ensure that safety measures are set in where the employee feels they can stop and talk things through at regular meetings or reviews are used to reinforce the employees' sense of worth and achievement. The employee then feels secure in admitting their own limitations and can more confidently work within them or stretch them with the safety of a helping hand. This goes for the leader too.

Case study comment

Getting to know self

"I do believe that everybody has authority. Living in communities you really do become to recognise the gifts and the leadership of each person in different areas. That person may not be the superior and in charge of the house, but if for example, I need someone to come out and help feed goats, I know exactly who I am going to ask, because that Sister has a giftedness with animals. She has the knowledge and intuitive sense about animals that perhaps I don't have. We call this 'authority', an authority that is authoring life, opening up a new awareness in others. When I work with her, I gain a lot, understand through her something new which is not natively mine to understand. It means that God gives each of us a certain capacity and giftedness, because of who we are, our geneology, past experiences and who our family is. It is up to us then to develop these talents. These become our set of gifts. As we develop those

▶

gifts more and more, people come to trust us in these areas. We are an 'authority', a kind of native authority. So I do believe the older we get the more we trust that in ourselves and the less that you try to pretend we're something else than we really are. We accept we have this talent and not that one. Then our authority has a certain resonance and people see us as a leader because we are really who we are, we have what we have been given and we don't try and act outside of our own essential gifts."

Sr. Judith Zoebelein, F.S.E., is a Franciscan Sister of the Eucharist, and founder of the Holy See's World Wide Web site on the Internet (www.vatican.va)

Education

Further training may be helpful in strengthening the employee to face their issues. Designing their development will give them extra ammunition against inevitable pressing and changing circumstances. Equally, pastoral support such as counseling can be educational in that it helps the employee realize the limitations they have and accept them.

Walk the talk

Apply EASE to ten of your employees throughout the company and formulate action plans for their coping with and predicting potential burn out.

Conclusion

Driving for success involves more than moving forward at one speed. To achieve the right level of push and pull toward the overall vision the great leader needs to perform an alchemous alliance between science and art. The scientific collection and analysis of data at different levels of the business is essential to accurate decision making and preventing molehills becoming mountains. This statistical performance management is then augmented by a holistic approach and the art of caring for the human being performing the tasks.

Once the correct balance of science and art is achieved and progress made toward the goal, further refinements are necessary in terms of ensuring a staying power for the leader, their team, and their systems. This includes embracing and accepting conditions such as burn out along the way as part of the performance process.

Great rate

This chapter has touched on some of the elements of "driving for success." It is not a definitive list but the elements which seem to make the difference involve:

Activity Based Calculators

Admit the Hit

Appraisal

Burn Out

Hard Line Audit

Key Performance Activities

Key Performance Indicator

Kinetic Performance Indicator

Limitation Low

Line Leader

Performance Measurement

Positive Psychological Policy

Soft Line Plaudit

Staying Power

CHAPTER 7

Developing leaders

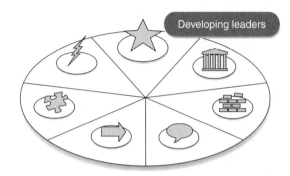

Source: Compiled by authors

Chapter introduction

Succession planning
A systematic approach which provides skills and leaders at all levels and may produce an overall leader grown from within

Career track development and support – others
Building structure, systems, and opportunities which ensure that potential leaders flourish

Talent retention
Having the strength to give talent in others the room to thrive and keeping ahead of their needs to keep them in the company

▶

Embracing diversity
Equitable approach to all potential leaders to tune into their "greatness." Embracing gender, ethnicity, age, religion as normal elements of talent make up rather than merely accommodating them

Career track development and support – self
Ensuring an organic and open approach to own development to keep own leadership appropriate to the needs of the follower and the organization

Deliberate direction – scalar of skills
Not leaving the development of self and others to evolve without a deliberate plan and direction to accrue the skill sets necessary to become not just a leader but a great leader

Once the portfolio of skills for the great leader are isolated, developed, and selected appropriately as each situation arises the increased likelihood of success is formed. Each leader can continue to refine their skills and ensure that they adapt more quickly to their followers and the situations which arise. Achieving corporate targets and competitive advantage is satisfying but only for a short term, if succession planning is not properly in place.

The development of followers is important at all levels to ensure success through increased output, quality and flexibility. These followers also need to be developed toward achieving a portfolio of leadership skills themselves so that they can lead at different levels of the business in the future. So, in addition to judging the levels of work and stimulation, the great leader must give careful thought and measured planning to ensure the provision of rounded skills development to produce future leaders from within. The next overall leader of the organization may then be organically grown and be able to progress the organization on a foundation of inside knowledge and experience.

To propagate these individuals, the right attitude and environment must be created within the organization and careful planning and career tracking as well as communication and controls are essential at all stages from Hatch to Despatch to create new leaders as well as refine the existing ones. Talent selection, talent management, and talent retention are important leadership skills in ensuring a robust enough platform for human growth as well as corporate growth. The leader's own capability comes into play here and they need a comfortable conscience of their own position. Talent attraction and propagation is not about one's own ego – it is more about letting that go, so good talent has the space it needs to flourish. Measurement and controls which are too restrictive may clip willing wings so the great leaders needs to proudly push forward talent from others giving it the appropriate acknowledgement in the open. The greatness comes from the grooming of that talent not the limiting of their enthusiasm, the snatching of their ideas, or claustrophobic control of their energetic influence on others in the company. Organizing the correct mix of mentoring and or coaching is essential, as is setting the right example to follow.

This takes us to the leaders themselves and their ongoing personal development so they serve their staff to their best ability. Developing leaders also start within. Is the leader ever really fully developed? Those that think they are may be fooling themselves. The leader who feels they must keep developing and adapting to different situations may have the longer shelf life.

Succession planning

Starting top down, the great leader needs to have an overall view of succession needs for their business or organization. There is little point in having a strategic plan which catapults the corporation forward if the necessary robust resources are not planned and secured. An overall view of staffing needs through means such as Training Needs Analysis (TNA) are useful in providing an umbrella to work beneath. More detailed planning and observation needs to be made at different levels in the company in order to isolate particular needs and work through likely outcomes of staff development.

Often the reality is more reactive than that and companies hurry and scurry to fill existing roles without the correct degree of homework. Previously decided hierarchies are refreshed with new "robotron" bodies and little proper study goes into realigning the roles to corporate needs or indeed to the needs of the talented individuals who already exist within the team.

A more proactive approach to succession planning is needed and this goes beyond merely working out who will take over from a particular manager or leader in a particular role. Of course, this is also essential and succession planning is built from within where daily working practices encourage a culture where things operate well, both efficiently and effectively when any manager or leader is away from the post. Leadership and management quality is judged by the ability to do this, not by the furrowed and self-important look over a constantly ringing mobile where staff constantly need overseeing. Appearing in constant demand and indispensable is now considered inefficient and ineffective. Colleagues and superiors can now see through the false protests at being disturbed and see that the participant is in fact indulging their own ego with a sideline strut.

This frontline approach to delegating and developing staff through day-to-day tasks is important and is an essential part of the overall but it will not in itself ensure appropriate level of succession planning to attain and retain competitive advantage. This must come from the top and work its way right through the layers of the organization.

A TNA can be done to provide a snapshot of the existing needs in the existing market. They are useful in that they do provide a fair representation of the training a company needs to put in straight away and this is a start to the succession planning process. The TNA can then provide a starting point and perhaps even a strong link between the individuals concerned, the teams they work in, and then the overall purpose. This though tends to be for that time and does not always differentiate between the short, medium, and long-term needs of the company.

Such studies should be broken down into these component parts to ensure that succession planning happens in the right way for all levels of business need vertically and also horizontally in terms of past, present and short, medium and long-term future.

Walk the talk

Look out your most recent TNA, or do one, and assess the current and future training needs of your business. Also, and at the same time, single out names of existing staff who may be suitable for progression planning within this.

Past

It is often tempting to brush away the past and deride past leaders when entering a new leadership role and looking to push toward the future. Much can be gained though from gracefully acknowledging the good work in the past and how it has contributed toward the picture today. Also many lessons can be learned, not just from any mistakes made, but from knowing that there is rarely anything ever really new and that the cycles of business have been encountered before – perhaps with a different name.

Past succession planning and experience will contribute to that of the moment and that of the future too. How strong corporate foundations are can be down to what was laid and how it was looked after. Remembering the past of an organization with affection can give a certain security to the current incumbents who will seek a foothold to be provided by the current leadership. One of those footholds can be the strength of the past. Characters of the past can be used to build a sense of history and belonging which gives more of a feeling of "permanentness." All too often, new brooms and fast change upset the staff layers and a temporary feeling is the result of the uncertainty. Creating this "permanentness" is not about setting a fixed rubric of behavior which will in itself become out of date quickly – it is more about setting in a reliability on and trust in others so the team can face change together, whatever that may be. Therefore, it is the trust and history together that is permanent – not the methods used.

This stability, certainty, and belonging gives more flexibility from within and that will show without. It caters for the current but also founds even more stable platforms for the future.

As well as respecting the past leadership for organizational interest, there is some sense in doing so for oneself as a leader. Every leader has a shelf life. We may be trying to extend that shelf life in this book by examining a portfolio of skills to mix and match accordingly but at some point one goes out of fashion and someone new comes in. If a culture of respecting past leaders has been set in place already it is more likely that our own "history" with the company is equally respected and used in its succession planning once our own time is up.

Present

As the snap shot, balance sheet information from observations and studies such as the TNA unfold, clear targets will be evident for skills development to tackle the present need. There is great value is a broad look at the development needs of the business at any given time to quickly fill any gaps.

To increase the value of this process for the present it is also wise to consider development across functions, areas, and so on so flexibility within is increased. Often gaps are filled but no real study of how staff movement within the organization can occur is made so sickness, and the like is covered as efficiently and effectively as possible. Such *succession spanning* is important at any moment in time but its ease of implementation and fluidity is only as good as the thought behind it. Having staff with the cross skills to cope with the needs of the day is a form platform of reactive robustness on which to build greater flexibility inside and out.

Walk the talk

Succession span your organization now. Who can work across functions easily and what are the "weak" areas in

> your business where if someone goes off sick or leaves, you
> will be vunerable?

Therefore, at any given moment in time a look at how fixed the
workforce is can be beneficial to the business. At the same time,
a Management Potential Analysis (MPA) can be performed so
future leaders and managers at different levels in the current pot
can be isolated. In fact, all management/leadership posts should
be mapped and assessed as to whether they have a successor in
tow and that the current training and development for them is
meeting their needs and that of the company.

With the data collection completed through TNAs or MPAs for
a "where are we now" look at the situation, it is then possible to
interweave a development plan for all levels of staff and future
leaders into the overall organizational direction, vision, and
strategy.

Future – short term

Short-term courses, conferences, and coaching can be planned
in to ensure the short-term leadership development needs of the
organization. Current leaders and managers throughout the
hierarchy need further grooming to maximize their potential,
keep them on the ball, and of course to help them move onwards
and upwards thus creating a healthy flow of personal growth
and talent throughout the company.

The short-term "freshening" of a dedicated course or workshop
also keeps the current management layers alert to issues at the
heart of the company. Going too long without these short-term
checks can mean managers and leaders get set in their ways and
stop looking for ways to improve. As all managers and leaders
know on every course you attend to develop one area of expertise, another area of expertise is highlighted for further work.
This stops complacency and ensures an ongoing look at personal development needs from the managers themselves as well
as those in charge of them.

It is the role of those in charge to link these short-term personal development needs to those short-term derivative targets from the vision and overall strategy. Just as KPIs and KPAs are assessed by observation, record, and variance analysis of the targets and actuals, so should the more holistic development needs of the individual. A variance analysis needs to be completed not just on the organizational need for skills through the TNA for instance, or even the MPA, but from the individual perspective of satisfaction and a real enrichment of their role and how it leads toward their leadership development.

Therefore, from *succession scanning, planning, and spanning*, we go to *progression planning and manning*. The difference between succession planning and progression planning is simply that the latter is not just about a reactive response to corporate needs but more a proactive action aimed at the individual first which then in turn benefits the organization anyway.

Walk the talk

Choose ten staff at different levels in your organization and assess their current progression plan with them either directly or through their line manager. Use previous appraisal and performance materials and evaluate how each delivers value to the guidance and motivation of that individual. Recommend how the performance process can be made as motivating as possible.

Work out the succession line beyond the immediate candidate for three posts for the next five years.

Future – medium term

Once areas for action have been isolated and short-term methods put in place, an infiltration into the real body of the organization is necessary to ensure the pathways for potential talent are opened and are available for those to shine. Time service here is not the qualifying criteria, talent is, and there will be those who will need a faster route forward than others. This should be thoughtfully accommodated to allow for it in the system in a positive way and where no resent is attracted and where no one feels left out.

Fast-track programs have their place and managed in properly can provide eager and energetic input from willing and hard-working staff who wish to give that bit extra to the norm.

This medium-term action need not be a corporate fast-track scheme, it could be an individual fast-track scheme where development programs are tailored to ability and aptitude, and progress the individual to a faster speed if they require it and less so if not. If the "contract" between appraiser and appraisee is agreed there should be no hard feeling for others who achieve more in less time if they are willing to put in the extra effort to achieve it.This changes the culture within from an aristocracy to a meritocracy.

Future – long term

While performance plates are spinning at different heights and speeds for the short and medium term, the great leader must plan for long-term *progression planning* and indeed consider long-term *progression manning*. Campaigns and schemes to attract new blood into the system are as important for the long-term future as ensuring the development and motivation of the existing workforce. Corporate graduate campaigns and development programs, or their like, set about satisfying this need and ensure a wave of fresh energy and opinion. Naturally, it is wise to expect that the attrition rate for these arrivals will be higher so planning should allow for a certain fallout level to ensure that a certain percentage of the candidates flow through the system.

This longer-term view looks beyond the immediate likely successor and invests in producing more likely successors for the future. Even where the leader is not involved with a corporate campaign to recruit the future wave of future leaders, it is still necessary to look beyond the need for the immediate successor and think several years hence at least.

The investment of a fresh wave of talent need not simply be at the classic graduate milk round end of the scale. Bulk attraction campaigns can be targeted at higher levels to create a new wave of possible senior leaders within the company. The NHS "Gateway to Leadership" Program is doing this at the point of writing where senior, experienced managers are being filtered through on line assessments, and the like, on a national basis.

Such attraction campaigns "herd hunt" rather than "head hunt" and create the greater likelihood of selecting the right leader.

On the subject of headhunting, which could be considered a shorter-term solution at point of action, the results of a longer-term succession planning process can bear fruit. Keeping an eye on figureheads and their herds in the competition is a long-term project that should be ongoing. Then if a short-term need arises action can be taken quickly with the long-term homework done.

Golden hellos are common at all new recruit attraction levels but particularly early intake levels to encourage the initial settling in. Staff benefiting from a several thousand pound golden hello are under contract to return it if they leave within a certain time. This approach has been used more widely in the past decade to attract staff into public sector work too – such as teachers.

Once these prize candidates and this wonderful pool of talent and potential are secured, the job is not finished. In fact, this is just the beginning in the striving to develop new leaders and ensure perpetual motion in the right direction. Once in the next priority is to try to keep them there.

Case study comment

Addressing the balance

"So I had responsibility for the personnel and for the training and quite a large number of staff in the organisation and worked very closely with the most senior officials. We did some really good things actually. For example, we still had at that point in NUPE swathes of male regional officials and very few women. We introduced a couple of things. Firstly, a very, very popular trainee officer scheme when we just went out and head hunted, for want of a better word, a whole lot of young women who we thought could make union officials and put them on a trainee scheme. They didn't necessarily have a union background but we brought them in and gave them, for a year, a kind of range of union experiences and then they were perfectly competent to be union officials. And that was a very good scheme and it was eventually copied by the TUC and is now an established part of union activity. We just pioneered it really. It was great because we began to transform people's concept of what a union official was like. You no longer had to be a kind of gruff man that shouted a lot and banged the table. It began to transform what union representation was about. So, I suppose I led that and got a lot of credit for that. And also we had all these male officials and then all the back room staff, the admin staff, the secretaries, the finance people were all women. So we started a scheme to try to give them the skills to become regional officials and cross that boundary, to encourage secretaries and admin staff to think of themselves as having a career path as a regional official and then possibly a national official and that worked really well as well. So both of these were good fun. I really enjoyed doing it."

Baroness Maggie Jones, House of Lords, ex-Unison

Career track development and support – others

Personal development plans (PDPs) are often referred to in current business climes. The fashionable focus is common but beneath the talk can often be found little substance. It is the responsibility of the leader to build a robust structure with reliable control systems to make a clear pathway for potential leaders to flourish.

Performance appraisal in some companies and institutions can be routine and token in nature. Managers and leaders can focus too much on performance measurement to tangible target rather than evenly mix in personal development for job enrichment. Appraisal forms from the previous year can be hurriedly scanned and objectives from them ticked or not with a reactive process drive rather than a proactive human drive.

Career track development for staff places the leader on a proactive footing where it is their duty to look ahead and even anticipate the career development needs of their staff. Career track development goes beyond performance management and wakes up what has become the predictable PDP. It is less about a list of desires and tailored actions, which are very valuable, let us not dilute their importance, and more about the proactive search for, or even creation of, opportunities, designed specifically for the individual. This approach gives them choice, direction, drive, satisfaction, and a reason to stay.

Case study comment

Individual attention and space

"I think our approach is that we really believe that the uniqueness of each person, that each of us is an unrepeatable part of creation and unless we seek to find our 'specialness' which is totally new, we are not able to understand the complexity of the world and our mission in it. Leadership for us is trying to understand that uniqueness in ourselves and others as related to any situation, bringing it into play with the people involved so that together what can offer to a situation a new mix and something creative can happen."

Sr. Judith Zoebelein, F.S.E., is a Franciscan Sister of the Eucharist, and founder of the Holy See's World Wide Website on the Internet (www.vatican.va)

The proactive career mapping also helps to fill future gaps in the hierarchy thus helping the business anyway. Even with the first focus on development of the individual, it is inevitable that in addition to development they will also volunteer to be "trained" in skills too to satisfy corporate need. Corporate-driven training and person-driven development can work hand in hand this way.

Equally important to this bottom-up approach is a top-down look the other way. A wise investment of time spent looking at all career tracks of all staff with and through line managers create the opportunity to discuss business needs through a people filter. Literally keeping a track on the career track will highlight areas for "anticipation" and the member of staff in receipt of a proactive approach will be more than pleasantly surprised at the foresight. The value of producing something before it is asked for also is that much greater for the homework done. Indeed, it is more and more clear that emotional perceptive ability is stronger for a little scientific planning and scanning.

The career track development should be a major part of the PDP process and that in turn a major part of the appraisal process. Once in place it is also self-perpetuating as the staff member willingly returns to the leader with feedback at agreed points and becomes more proactive themselves in their own future. This is an important step in terms of developing future leaders as getting them to do more and more from within will produce a stronger and more versatile character as well as one more able to think ahead for others in an altruistic and empathic manner.

In addition to fulfilling the staff member and enriching their employment, the development for the future approach is more than likely going to increase their tenure with the establishment. This in turn will increase their intimate knowledge of the company and this could contribute to the quality of their future leadership decision making.

Case study comment

Pride in pushing others on

"I learnt and it reinforced the belief that I'd always had that most of the people, most of the time, have enormous

▶

amounts of common sense and that there is a whole raft of people out there who, because of their life chances have not had a chance to get a better paid job or to progress, but actually if you give them the chance they can go much further than their current situation would lead you to believe. So, the great thing about the union, the great thing about the women that we organised, was that you could see them grow before your eyes. They could be middle aged, they could be in their 50s, the union gave them a chance to find a whole new world where they would get their confidence, they could learn new skills, work their way right up to the top so that some of them, who were great women, ended up being the President and leading the union and speaking at TUC and Labour Party and I felt an immense sense of pride in all this. They were just a privilege to work along side in many ways. So it reinforced my belief in human beings and their potential to grow."

Baroness Maggie Jones, House of Lords, ex-Unison

Talent retention

By deliberately tracking personal careers and developing staff appropriately for themselves and the company, a culture of valuing talent is formed and most likely further cultivated. This should retain that same talent within the company and secure their even more valuable, willing, and energetic efforts. The career tracking produces a firm framework to work around and a tangible and visible direction to devote to. Retaining talent in this way does then strengthen the company. There is more though than this framework to ensure if this approach is to be successfully followed by the leader. Creating the way forward for each individual vision is an important part of the whole vision but becomes merely a process or lip service if it is not accompanied by a certain level of belief and altruism.

It takes a certain type of leadership strength to devote to others and give them the room they need to thrive. When looking after the needs of the talent within, the leader will not only produce longer serving individuals who are happier in their roles but also perhaps uncover different talents and even better talents to their own. The spirit of true talent retention means any discomfort or insecurity must take second place to the needs of the company and this talent should be encouraged and retained without direct comparison to self. The leader's own level of talent in a certain area should not be the capped point at which everything stops. The leader should feel relaxed enough to allow the complete fulfillment of that individual to their point of saturation – not the leader's own – even if that means the leader stepping back as a facilitator and becoming a coach rather than a mentor – in fact especially if this is the case. It is more about pushing the individual to their own peak performance by drawing it out of them than merely showing an example and passing on the expertise of the leader themselves.

It takes a particularly strong belief in oneself to be confident to help those around us with different and sometimes greater talent. Allowing the room for different creativity and different talent is as uncomfortable as allowing a staff member to excel more than yourself in a particular area. However, the alternative is to place a ceiling over it and/or clip it back to a comfortable shape and subsequently deny the organization the talent it needs to thrive. There will not be many reading this book that have not met just such a so-called leader whose own agenda dictated the level to which all others were allowed to achieve under their reign.

Great leadership does not just allow the room for the talent but also encourages it with a true sense of pride in any progress made. The great leader keeps the accreditation for new ideas and achievements attached to the original source and takes their satisfaction from being the facilitator and propagator while they ensure that the source of the talent gets the glory. So many times in organizations, it is heard that superiors take direct credit for a subordinate's work. It is clearly time for this archaic practice to cease. Real leadership is not that insecure and trusts that there is greater satisfaction, and yes if you like glory, in standing back and pushing someone else forward.

This is extra important as it is fair to say that talented staff tend to come with high egos and need them feeding regularly. They may also be more maverick in nature and/or not quite conform to a certain pattern of recruit in the company. This may also mean they naturally aggravate others without doing that much and conflict can occur in teams who are uncomfortable with a different character. Therefore, in addition to managing the actual talent and allowing them the room to thrive, there is a further responsibility for the great leader to ensure their safe and settled introduction into a team.

Talent jealousy is not confined to the previously mentioned leaders with wing clippers. Talent jealousy can also occur at "sibling" level and indeed can be even worse in terms of its internal destruction of the productive working environment. The introduction of a new, more or differently talented member into a team at peer level may cause some in the existing team to feel worried about how they compare which can then lead to political sniping and worse. The great leader will have anticipated such reaction and help introduce and retain the new talent by ensuring neutrality and support for all. Wise and experienced leaders of talent diversity will ensure that the team work together with the existing and new talent and take responsibility for any team dynamic failure. Organizations can often lose the wrong people because of such politics – particularly where they occur at an underground level. It is down to the leader to ensure the right staff are retained and not working for the competition instead as moving is easy for talented candidates. This is less of a problem if the talented member enters at a higher level with the power to make changes and in a position less likely for direct attack from any sibling type jealousy.

Of course, it is also possible for the leader to be landed with less talented recruits and these are less likely to move – simply because they will not get loads of offers elsewhere. There are some practices though where companies have been known to encourage the headhunting of certain staff because they are weaker and knowing these weaker staff are in the competition is reassuring!

Put simply the leader is judged on their retention and effective management of talent and they are judged by the quality and performance of their team. These things are important measures and rate alongside profit, and so on when evaluating the leadership skills level and performance level.

Embracing diversity

As part of developing leaders at all levels of the business, including oneself, the great leader has a core responsibility to ensure an equitable approach to all potential leaders. Tuning into the components of each person's "greatness" will increase the levels of the right leadership within the organization. In addition to the previously mentioned talent management and retention where tall flowers standing higher than the rest of the field are not clipped back but encouraged to shine, there is the matter of ensuring the real embracing of gender, ethnicity, age, and religion as normal elements of that talent make up. Many accommodate diversity and follow legislation to the letter, but this is more than that – it is about getting to know the whole person and the important things which influence their lives and understanding how that influences their work and attitudes to change.

The gender arguments have changed considerably in the past few years. With more acknowledgment for emotional qualities being part of a successful leader's package of skills alongside analytical ones, it has become more recognized that each can bring their own strengths to the equation. Equally, it is never as simple as gender division anyway as within each gender category lies many levels of ability and aptitude for analysis and empathy.

That is not to say that glass ceilings have been removed. Of course, there will still be places where they do exist and there will still be the inevitable effects of previous male dominated cultures and histories. However, women have started to realize that it is not necessarily the current male who is their competitor, it is the inherited culture itself. No one is saying that is right and that women have not had their wings clipped by practices in the past and indeed that it will not happen as an inherited habit in the future. It is clear though that it is not for the current male population to be made to pay for that past and that all participants have inherited its legacy.

The evening out process in the past few decades has been interesting. Such has been the focus on improving the lot of the female, whole new issues of gender identity have been brought to the fore in the new millennium. Where woman are gaining ground in some areas and cultures changing to allow them the flexibility they need to pursue their own goals at work, it could be said that some ground for young males has been lost in that they find it difficult to know what their role now is. The current generation of female worker and future leader has had a better deal than her mother and grandmother in many ways and gender mixes are changing to the point where women are now a significant proportion of the workforce, so it follows that their needs must be catered for by leaders. Mind you, regardless of proportion, these needs should be met. Meritocracies are more likely now and women leaders do not want to gain anything through favor or tokenism. Being the token female on a Board is not an achievement – gaining the place through talent is.

Competition for women in the workplace need not necessarily come from men any more, in fact, it is likely that competition or grief may come from another female. New waves of future female leader are entering workplaces where older generations of women regard them as having a much easier time. There is some sympathy when some of those women have had to make choices between having families for instance because the culture was different then. There is no sympathy though when they block the way of an up and coming female because of resent.

In addition, female competition is only something that other females can really understand the intricacies of. It could be said that in all women there still remains the genetic need to be the one "chosen" over and above the others, the one who metaphorically gets dragged to the cave by her hair as such. This natural *one-up-womanship* manifests itself in many ways and at many levels in the workplace and needs to be understood by the leader so attentions can be equitably distributed to ensure a greater level of harmony.

This applies more practically as well as emotionally as it is important to manage organizational understanding and flexibility carefully. It is only fair to ensure a certain flexibility for those with families but leaders have to ensure that such gender provision does not actually turn inwards on the section of staff whom they are trying to help. For instance why should the "singles" get landed with working the Christmas stints – isn't their Christmas just as important as any other? These house-keeping matters really do need to be sorted fairly and sensitively as they can build up resent over time if not handled well.

In any case, the modern female worker, whether a mother or not, wants an equitable flexibility without being made a special case. It is only right that she wants her achievements to be rec-ognized for what they are – not something achieved by way of a favor from the system. This way a truer *meritocracy* is achieved and peer credibility is a constant and normal currency.

This is not to say that some extra pressures are not there for women and that provision should not be made to assist them in their ability to work in a fair arena, just that it should be a natu-ral part of leadership to manage this diversity along with others. Its practice should be so absorbed in the course of normal events as not to be instantly distinguishable. Leadership which assesses situations and success by output rather than specific input can often be better suited to manage gender diversity. A manager with their eye on every minute of the clock is simply monitoring levels of presenteeism and does not necessarily achieve synergy or willing effort. Indeed the extra tension created can actually turn things the other way. If the calculation of success is that which is actually produced and willingly given the leader may promote more effort above and beyond the call of duty from a more respectful subordinate.

The leader can help avoid tension and awkward situations by thinking through systems, routines, and rituals within the organization. It may be that holding meetings at a certain time of the day inadvertently discriminates against those who have the school run on their agenda and varying the times these meet-ing are held may be more equitable. Cultures of consideration can be cultivated from the top downwards in this way so smaller daily practices complement the diversity of the workforce rather than hinder it. Interestingly, it is often the small things that can cause the most aggravation and this accumulates over time to build up resent if the leader does not take the time to look out for it.

"Presenteeism" cultures are being replaced by "present the goods" cultures so that "noise" is replaced by "action."

On the flip side, there are areas where the great leader can set about assisting men in their pursuit for equality too. Some corporate cultures impede the free expression of their male staff by setting a rubric of certain male behavior within the working environment. For instance, in some organizations it is still awkward to actually take your full paternity leave even though it is there by law. Thankfully, this is changing but it is a good example of how practice or culture can actually influence a staff member's rights and make them feel differentiated for the wrong reason.

In the same way, such practices can be ageist. Certain age groups of staff may have more responsibilities outside of the workplace and be subject to more pressure, not just from children but also from elderly parents. The support within the leadership of this element of diversity is important to show the value of the staff undergoing the issues. After all, the same well-mortgaged family person is likely to be a reliable, hardworking, and trustworthy asset to a company so it is only fair that their human needs are understood in a seamless way which does not make them stand out or feel lesser. Even well meaning social rituals such as the happy hour for staff at the local wine bar can accidentally exclude those with other demanding agendas.

Imbalances in the ages of team members can by default cause isolation. A younger person joining an older established team or an older person joining a younger team can experience a certain misfit and will not necessarily be able to cope on their own with the segregation. Leaders have a responsibility to close the gaps in terms of familiarization exercises and support either way to prevent any quiet departures. Not everyone will admit the real reason for leaving when situations like this occur in case it makes them sound a bit "no mates" but it is something quite easily spotted ahead if one makes the effort to look.

Some issues may be evident if the leader themselves is younger than some of their staff, particularly if that leader has been promoted over and above an existing experienced member. In this classic case, the leader must ensure room is given for pride to be maintained. Being modest enough to openly seek advice from the older candidate will restore their standing in the work community and maintain their sense of worth. This use of personality power rather than clumsier positional power will also gain more respect from that individual. In this way, the leader is not only increasing the working trust of their team members but also benefiting from the experience of the individual which in turn helps both parties develop into better leaders for the company.

Developing self and future staff into better leaders also involves embracing the wonderful wealth of cultural and religious difference across all ethnicities. One does not need to know every difference intimately but more have an open mind and respect for them. If some flexibility in working patterns is possible for certain festivals such as Eid and Divali, then this demonstrates that they are as important as other more commonly celebrated times. There are no rules but a demonstrated respect and fairness across the Board will help to maintain the right core values in the organization for example. Staff will tend to copy what they see from the top so it is essential that he leadership example crosses the range of staff in the team.

Respect for the cultural and religious beliefs of staff then becomes an inherited spirit and future leaders develop a broader view and tolerance of the diversity around them. Even where some come to the company with more restricted backgrounds limiting their tolerance of the difference in others, a culture or respect within the organization and sported by the leader will quickly teach them different norms and make them better leaders for the future which is obviously going to be more diverse anyway.

In the same way that age can isolate some members from groups, so can ethnicity and religion. It therefore becomes one of the key responsibilities of the leader to evaluate the needs of their diverse staff framework in advance and make every effort to ensure they work as well as possible together. In addition to setting the right atmosphere and attitudes from their example, the leader must also facilitate team bonding and inclusion and make particular efforts where they may anticipate a problem.

Beyond the familiar aspects of diversity which every great leader sets out to get as right as possible, there are also the more hidden ones within the teams. Less obvious diversity dilemmas may lie outside of skin color, gender, age, and so on and manifest from core personalities in the groups and teams. Different backgrounds and experiences, different approaches, different characters, and even different classes such as they still exist now, may cause political elements within the working structure. Staff can feel irritated by someone different to them in terms of personality or perhaps even threatened by a new, energetic, lively team member. This diversity is also the responsibility of the leader to help with and they have a duty to prevent issues where possible and mediate them fairly where they do occur.

Career track development and support – self

Ensuring an organic and open approach to own development to keep own leadership appropriate to the needs of the follower and the organization is therefore essential. Personal development for the great leader never stops if they are to remain ever responsive to change and be the right leader for each staff member relying upon them. A rounded leadership capability development is a core responsibility if one has the privilege of serving followers.

It can be the case that top-level leaders reach a final place of "made it" and heavily rely on positional power and experience to effect what they feel to be appropriate changes and directives. More is likely to be gained from ensuring an ongoing self-development spirit in terms of how the leader serves others. Rather than become complacent with set styles, or in some cases, one style, it serves the business and the staff better if the leader constantly seeks development to refine their styles and increase their abilities of perception, approachability, analysis, and so on. Indeed, increase their capabilities of resilience, strategic thinking, decision making, and team work at a senior level while ensuring the highest levels of integrity.

Case study comment

Personal progress under pressure

"For me, it just forced me to have a new range of skills, confidence skills. You have to be able to get up and speak in public. You have to get up on a platform and persuade people. Whereas, I suppose, people might have thought I was a relatively shy student, you know, shy and quiet. But you learnt that you had to be bolshy quite quickly. So I learnt those sorts of skills. I didn't learn the traditional management skills I wouldn't have said at that point."

Baroness Maggie Jones, House of Lords, ex-Unison

Revitalizing one's own approach regularly will address the core responsibility to others and inject a freshness into the day-to-day activities and processes. Not only will this improve the quality of the activities but also the freshness is catching and will cascade down the system. It sets a good example to others and they will be the fresher and more enthusiastic for it.

Apart from going on various courses and reading a good healthy range of leadership material, business publications, and so on the leader can gain a lot from discussing through the training and personal development of others in their team. Even sitting in on some of the courses the staff attend under the guise of a quality measure or in most cases genuine interest, is a good way of learning oneself – without admitting you do not know something or being shown up!

The great leader must not only keep fresh but also keep ahead and that is why they should have their own PDP which incorporates a greater span of time into the future than that of their subordinates. In fact, it is not a bad idea to sum up the training and development within the hierarchy of one's span of control and perform a TNA on oneself. This gap analysis then will automatically give the particular action points for one's own PDP as

well as being tailored to business need. Consider it as an arm of
the strategic plan. It is not just what is planned for the business
and the people within it but also for oneself to make sure of
delivery.

Walk the talk

Do just that. Produce a sum of the training and development within your span of control and further, and assess
your capability to oversee this. From your gap analysis produce an action plan tailored to these needs and line it up
with your vision.

The development of leadership capability then is not only developing all of the skills outlined in these chapters but then applying
them in the right mix to ensure that as the leader one is in the best
position and has the best ammunition to make the best decisions
for the company and its people. Leadership capability involves
ensuring a level of personal resilience great enough to carry the
business forward and for staff to believe in as well as making strategic decisions work at operational levels. The same capability
has to stretch from ensuring effective team dynamics at senior
level right down to the frontline. Although there are top-level
courses to cater for such leadership grooming, the real development is gained from actually doing it and of course making the
mistakes. True leadership development of self and true cultivation of capability comes then from being able to admit those mistakes and learn from them. It comes from being approachable
and able to listen to the workforce while ensuring the build up of
trust as followers can rely on a certain high level of integrity.

Deliberation direction – scalar of skills

With a number of essential areas to master on the leadership
front, not just to become as great as one can as a leader but also

to master the skills which are essential just to get by, there needs to be a master plan. A deliberate direction of stages and events needs to be mapped out for each prospective and current leader so these skills can be obtained – proactively not just reactively.

The route map to development already exists within the current hierarchy so as well as planning the development progress of each individual according to their needs and matching those with the corporate need, it is also a very good idea to helicopter over the hierarchy to map out the opportunities which will arise within. In addition to this, the great leader would also set certain leadership skills targets to be gained at certain levels so all potential leaders are driven toward a rounded set of skills and pushed into the appropriate arenas to gain them. This drive ensures that by the time certain hierarchical levels are reached, certain skills can be counted on and deliberate action has been taken to expose the individuals to the experiences they need to pass this mark.

Such a corporate and structural approach added to the individual tailoring approach will ensure that all angles are covered to propagate the great – propagreat!

This propa-great-ion involves a scalar of skills lined up with each hierarchical levels and the sum of these then accumulates to form a rounded skills set worthy of a great leader.

Following the elliptical guide of the model used in this book, the scalar skills for each of the seven sides of great leadership will appear at different levels.

Being great

It could be said that "greatness" can be spotted early on at lower levels, or at least the capacity to be so. This then is groomed to greater greatness by experience of events as leaders work their way through the hierarchy and are encouraged to take on more and stretch themselves. This greatness must start with a passion for the detail and the frontline of the business and then be added to as experience is gained. Starting one's greatness at task/operation level ensures a grasp of the real core of activity, a chance to "feel" the needs of the customer at the frontline and of course a chance to view the management and leadership prowess of one's superiors. A lot can be learned from those who lead and manage badly.

Crafting the future

The skills needed to be able to craft the future can be developed from the first line management role any leader takes on. It is at this level, with responsibility for one or several staff, that teeth can be cut to gain this particular and very important skill. At this lower line management level the leader is fed the essentials of the overall vision in a translated form to suit them. There is a clear opportunity for their superior and indeed themselves to contextualize their vision meaning and learn the art of telescoping it through different levels. Mentoring and coaching support from the overall leader is essential here to reinforce – not only the message – but also the methods through which they are delivered.

It is also important at this stage to ensure that staff have opportunities early in their careers to work with high level and top managers so that they grasp the importance of the overall future and vision and see for themselves how that translates to their work. Once this shadowing is achieved, the student leader in question is always aware of the totality of the organization and takes this through everything they do as they progress in the organization.

In essence it is not only the future of the organization that is crafted here but the skill of crafting the future which is also crafted in the up and coming leader of the future.

Surfacing sentiments

Once a manager progresses to unit level and more people then exist between them and the frontline, situations where they will not be in direct contact with their frontline staff will be common. It is at this point they will have to grow antennae and find different and nondirect methods of surfacing sentiments. They will need to refine their approachability to ensure that they are open to suggestions and opinion and mechanically work out the right communication supports. Success in this area is a real growth milestone as it is beyond finding the ability to directly impact a situation through instruction and realizing the finesse of impact and influence through other indirect means. Essential at this point are executive level courses which not only look at scientific techniques of leadership but also analyze the impact of psychological and emotional methods.

Developing these emotional skills takes time and of course exposure. Leaders need the opportunities to be able to evolve the necessary emotional approachability but also, and very importantly, the necessary emotional toughness and resilience to cope. Having the ability to pitch the right emotional output to a staff member during performance-oriented feedback is key as is having the strength and thickness of skin to soak up the frustrations and tensions of others. Being able to raise more uncomfortable issues in the right constructive way is also something which needs to be developed. Psychological profiling can help leaders realize their default tendencies and highlight areas for further work or concentration to make them more rounded and appealable to their followers.

1. Finding ways through
2. Engaging
3. Driving for Success

By divisional management level, these three areas of the great leader really come into play. Some of the prior development mentioned will act as a foundation but it is now essential that management support mechanisms are available for leaders to discuss projects and situations. They also need the vehicle to thrash out more strategic intentions and to be furnished not just with an active democratic and vibrant environment in which to ensure that they get all the information and opinion they need but also the strategic overview support from the Board level.

This should be further supported by a more sophisticated level of learning and perhaps study so broader ability is gained.

Being able to furnish a more refined level of communication with staff respecting cultural and ethical influences while being able to competently design appropriate structures to underpin the overall vision is no easy ask. Some trial and error is inevitable but less loss will result if gearing is toward positive development and discussion and these skills are encouraged and supported. Sharing expertise and seeking opportunities to stretch self and others is essential.

To be able to do this the progressing leader needs to keep refining their perceptive abilities so that they can be in tune with others. Learning to look for signs and getting to know their staff is important so changes are easily spotted. This enables the leader to fully engage with the follower and change their mind set.

As well as having this increased awareness developed, there is also the question of durability. The leader, to drive for success must develop the stamina to cope. They need the energy and commitment to the cause and cannot flag if they wish to have continued success. Knowing one's capability is essential so realism can be put into the planning equation as can PDPs and psychological profiling which increase endurance as well as awareness.

Developing leaders

At Board level, the development of self and others becomes a prime responsibility so a causal loop of greatness is created. Nothing is left to accident and deliberate plans set in place to ensure exposure to events which give the rounded experience necessary from the start through all the levels of responsibility. This will broaden the decision-making ability right throughout the ranks and create multidisciplinary teams where talent is spotted, fully utilized and pushed to its most effective limits.

Such approaches will ensure that individuals develop clusters of skills they can draw on in situational context. This strengthens not the leadership choices they make in those situations but gives each individual more choice as to how they progress in the company. This in itself is more likely to increase the levels of retention and satisfaction which will then be fed back into the organization in many positive ways.

All levels will contain opportunities to gain all of the skills necessary for the seven sides of great leaders but it is fair to comment that by certain stages, certain of these skills should be present and prerequisite to the next progression step. Figure 7.1 shows this clearly and once achieved these skills are then taken to the next level and added to. Only by deliberately ensuring that these skills are experienced and gained will the individual arriving at Board level be really prepared for what is ahead of

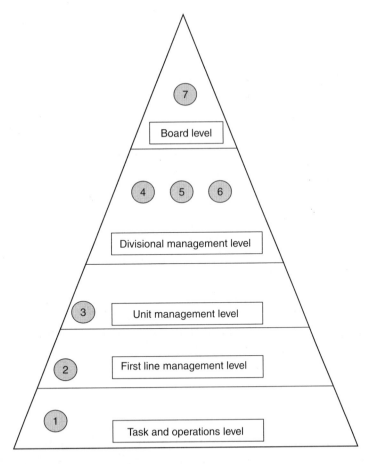

Figure 7.1   Scalar of skills

Source: Authors

them. Only with this skills underpinning can they really serve their followers in the best way and create a cycle of development to strengthen the organization from within.

Therefore, having traveled through the corporate layers, it can be seen that a pattern emerges in terms of skills, core competencies, and subsequent core capabilities. Level 1 is about the basic skills which form the base on which to develop leadership core competencies at levels 2 and 3. Once these are in place they can be used and adapted in many ways becoming core capabilities at 4, 5, 6, and 7. By this point leadership ability and capability is much more sophisticated and in a state of much more ready adaptability because of that.

Conclusion

Developing leaders involves so much more than establishing a recruitment and development campaign to ensure a healthy through put. Appropriate recruitment plans need supporting performance management support which come not just in the form of formal procedures but in the form of genuine and tailored human interest for each individual. Add to this an open minded and healthy respect for each individual's differences in terms of their personality, ability, ethnicity, gender, age, family circumstance, religion, and so on and we start getting somewhere close to really developing that individual into a future leader. The carefully thought out development for the leader themselves and ensuring this is ever refreshed by up-to-date material which keeps them open minded and forward thinking will underpin the structural and pastoral partnerships. This way future leaders are not only grown but are also better prepared for the many changes they have in front of them. This way development is deliberate and not accidental.

Great rate

This chapter has touched on some of the elements of "developing leaders." It is not a definitive list but the elements which seem to make the difference involve

▶

Career Track Development

Embracing Diversity

Hatch to Despatch

Management Potential Analysis

Meritocracy

Progression Manning

Progression Planning

Scalar of Skills

Succession Planning

Succession Scanning

Succession Spanning

Talent Retention

Training Needs Analysis

Total leadership – forever refreshed

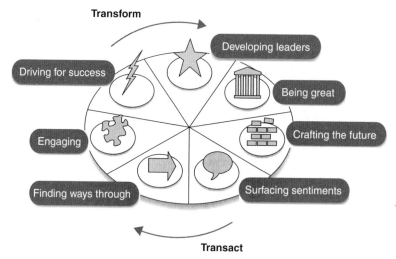

Source: Authors

The journey through the seven chapters of great leadership brings us to a full circle. With each of the sides looked at in relative detail, it is clear that each side can be taken off the shelf as needed and/or combined with one or two of the other skills to provide a suitable combination of skills for the situation facing the leader at that moment. The approach has been one of tailoring, one of adapting, and one of pushing for passionate self-improvement to serve followers in the way they need it. Ultimately, this increases the shelf life of the leader and increases the competitive advantage of the organization they work for.

The approach of this book has very much been one of roundedness and it is interesting that in the journey through the seven sides we have come full circle in developing others to become great as well as be more great ourselves. This 360-degree causal loop is never left and the great leader travels it and uses it – in perpetuity.

This globalization is an inner globalization – the globalization of different parts of the inner world of leadership which are brought together not just within the individual but within the organization. Inner globalization is the mirrored reflection of outer globalization which is the outer facing front of the organization and its position in the world market. Increasingly easy links with other countries makes expansion and supplier and customer sourcing something which can reach further corners. This brings extra and even more exciting challenges to the great leader wanting to be even greater. New skills must be learned to cope with leading in different cultures, in different circumstances, and over different distances. Remote leadership is necessary and brings with it extra areas for consideration as direct contact with teams and individuals becomes less frequent or nonexistent. Motivational techniques and methods for keeping all in line with the strategic direction have to be adapted to serve the followers through more complicated communication channels.

Inner globalization

Starting with self, the inner ellipse of excellence is something the great leader is in constant pursuit of. Acquiring or developing the necessary analytical, emotional, and communication skills necessary for success is a part of a never ending journey of improvement and a foothold to higher and more sophisticated levels of leadership application. Once acquired, the individual skills need to be subjected to the appropriate alchemy to produce the right combination for the events of the moment. Rounding off this ability to judge the right skills set at the right time in the right dose is the route to the greatness sought and leadership judgment and discretion is ever refreshed and refined to achieve this. The great leader sets out to achieve the best inner worldliness possible so that parochial and set thinking is abandoned for wider and more flexible thought and action.

The same worldly approach is necessary at team level too. It is also the duty and the target of the great leader to ensure that their teams are prepared for all types of events to come as well as those which line up with the vision now. Just as there must be an inner globalization of self, the teams must be inner globalized to form their own resilience and levels of flexibility. This may be achieved by valuing the diversity of the actual skills within and managing them and leading them to synergetic outcome. It may also be achieved through focusing on the individuals within that team as well as what they produce as a whole body and isolating the development they need on a tailored basis for them which adds to the whole team and corporate vision. Such rounding off of each team or unit will have the benefit of adding flexibility to that team and they will help and understand other teams and units in the organization. This will strengthen the roots of the company and also create further opportunity for the individuals within the teams as they can move around the organization more freely, not just assisting it but developing themselves in the process.

This also applies to the whole organization which should be able to look in on itself and assess its level of inner globalization. The roundedness of the organization as a whole should reflect, as well as be reflected in, the individual and team levels of flexibility. With the ability to draw on the resources necessary for the moment, the organization can then adapt the right form, literally, to face oncoming change. Being able to do this more speedily and with the right resource mix is a clear competitive advantage.

The spirit of this text is to discuss the skills and tools necessary to achieve the maximum inner globalization possible for most effective performance through appropriate and tailored leadership chosen for the benefit of the company and its situation at the time – not the individual recruited into the key position.

Inside or out, it is clear that successful leadership is never truly mastered as it is an organic service which must be ever refreshed and refined. The changing nature and demands of the follower and the changing nature and demands of the external environment mean that even once the leader has reached a point of maximum provision for their troops in their current state, they must put some serious planning into the next likely situation they will face. There is no rest, learning to lead never stops and the truly successful, the truly great leader knows that they are leading to learn.

So how does the great leader keep themselves forever refreshed so they can ensure all of this?

Following the elliptical guide of the model used in this book, there are things the leader can do for every side of being a great whether by using check points or developing a deliberate point of reinvigoration.

Being great

Perhaps the real secret to being great in terms of ever refreshing is to never actually think that you are great. If greatness is approached as the building of confidence, knowledge, and skills from within and is a constant journey of self-improvement rather than an arrived at destination then the resulting humility and modesty will not only open eyes to other self-fulfilling journeys but also make the leader more approachable, likeable, and perhaps then more admired and respected.

Being great is in the eyes of the beholder and they are less likely to think so if you think you are too great. That is not to say that a certain level of confidence should not be exuded, as it is important that the troops believe in your ability to take the company forward but that it should be twinned with humility to ensure a level of endearment from those followers. This will secure their trust and extra energy and this extra willing effort will improve results which will in turn make you, the leader, appear more great in the eyes of the shareholders and the Board.

This open and humble attitude will serve well in terms of attracting opportunities to refresh and as well as something from within, a realization that greatness is a sum of different skills too – appropriately applied – will ensure a never ending and open minded elliptical journey through the different sides. This will furnish the great leader with a greater chance of getting it right first time as the chances that their decision will be accurate will be greater and this in turn will add to that greatness.

Crafting the future

The secret to ever refreshing the skill of crafting the future must lie in a mix of constant improvement and satisfaction as to what is arrived at and achieved. The simple act of crafting the future is not enough in itself. It has already been seen that the overall target is broken down into component and understandable parts at different levels. This would suggest that there are many opportunities for refreshing the skill. The attempts to translate the vision to the troops will result in a mix of successes and failures. Using these failures as positive learning processes in an open discussion with others will refresh the efforts the next time a similar situation arises.

Similarly knowing when to be satisfied is key, although one never stops questioning whether there could be a slight better way round things the next time. Being openly happy and praising about achievements will encourage the effort from others again and refinements can be introduced in subtle and constructive ways.

Disciplining oneself to scenario plan in wider ways will also increase the coverage of possible future happenings – so that when more unexpected events do occur some discussion or thought has been made in that area which will help progress.

In addition to concentrating on the delivery of the vision at different levels in different languages to different audiences, the great leader would get much from looking at the vision itself, as well as its many component parts, from different angles. This way their outlook remains fresh and subsequently so do they.

Surfacing sentiments

Being able to surface true sentiments at surface and sub surface level takes as much scientific homework as it does natural empathy with others –, that is, if one agrees that empathy is natural rather than a sum of more alert observation. Perhaps the more alert observation arrives as a result of the more in-depth homework. Refreshing this skill involves an alchemy of people and science. Knowing histories and facts about staff can make anticipation of their needs more accurate. This skill could be refreshed by ensuring that the data supply on all staff is refreshed regularly by deliberate research expeditions. Being curious and getting out to talk to staff contextualize so much of what happens in the business and why and helps build up bonds which attract the trust levels necessary for a real level of communicative understanding where real feelings are shared.

The scientific collection of data is then refreshed at a different level by the leader working on their levels of approachability. This can only be practiced and reflected upon. The proof will be in the levels of trust displayed by the staff. Even when this is achieved though, it is fair to say that complacency may set in and ruin things. Therefore, it is necessary to refresh the knowledge of that trust and understanding regularly so all are reassured of its presence. It is also important to really value the view of the business through the eyes of a fresh individual with a different angle on matters and equally as important to have the sheer resilience to cope with the views given. Being able to take constructive criticism and welcome opposite views as well as cope with the quantity of opinion takes a certain strength but delivers a certain value. Such value can bring a different perspective to the decision-making equation – not to mention the forward planning.

Finding ways through

Hard structural design, outsourcing, remote management, ethical and cultural soft structures bring a very diverse challenge to the leader aiming for greatness. So many areas in which to gain expertise and then on top of that ensure each of them is refined and refreshed.

Here a good method for reinvigoration is to make comparative studies of other organizations so lessons can be learned and new ideas considered. Other organizations who have had the challenges of outsourcing may be able to advise against certain pitfalls so clear advantages can be gained. This way – the way through is refreshed by the learning and experience of others as well as the level of ability of the leader. Here also, being open to and willing to embrace change and new ideas will increase the leader's ability to renew their own approach to the way forward.

Engaging

True engagement takes leadership skills to deeper levels of understanding and working through others. Achieving the real buy in from followers involves gaining their physical input as well as their ideas. Delegating them duties which further develop their abilities is a further skill which helps furnish this and this too can revitalize the input at the core of the organization. In addition to refreshing the list of delegates for different duties to round off the pool of experience available, the leader can refresh their own methods of instruction so each task has that extra energy and fails to become a routine request delivered by way of habit. If duties are requested in such a way then they will be completed with the same spirit. Given a fresh and positive objective, the follower will respond in the same way. It is all too easy to cop out of injecting that extra energy into a requested task but the results will speak for themselves either way. Equally, the leader can deliver their feedback and constructive criticism in such a way as to ensure the personal development of those entrusted with the responsibilities in hand.

Driving for success

Performance monitoring and management may be necessary in terms of gathered data and holistic care of followers, but again there are opportunities to ensure such things do not get stale. Many leaders work from the same repetitive management information – making major decisions based on what they see. The mechanical tools can also be refreshed by looking at matters from different perspectives and focusing on different cost, sales, and service drivers. This new angle will refresh decisions. Pastoral matters can also become routine and waste golden opportunities to find out about people and retain them. Appraisal procedures for instance can be used to really get to know staff rather than routinely tick boxes. The leader's approach to implanting these and following them up can make all the difference to their impact at all levels.

Developing leaders

This all adds up to continuous development. Interestingly, aside from the definite ways in which one can use courses and opportunities to develop, it is clear that an attitude and open mindedness is key to further development so renewal, refreshing, and revitalizing are constant items on the agenda. Being willing to attend different types and different levels of training and discussion will help open up new ideas and information to the leader which will obviously refresh their work, but not as much as being constantly open to those new inputs as a matter of course rather than just going on a course.

This energetic and positive attitude will infect others and they will go on to self-renew as a matter of course. The great leader does not just reinvent their own methods, they reinvent others.

And so back to side 1 – being great. It is clear how all sides interlink. It is clear how all sides can mix and match. It is clear that being great involves having all sides ready to use and knowing when to use them and in what mix. It is clear that being great is about doing this as a willing duty to others and gaining respect through hard-earned work for followers. It is clear that real greatness is worked hard for but not "worn" like a medal with pompous pride. It is a humble achievement, worn with modesty and an attitude that there is always more to learn and improve upon.